RETURN OF THE SWASTIKA?

KW-946-324

By the same author

The Scourge of the Swastika
Though the Heavens Fall
The Knights of Bushido
That Reminds Me
If I Forget Thee
The Royal Conscience
The Trial of Adolf Eichmann
The Tragedy of the Congo
South Africa Today—and Tomorrow?
The Knight of the Sword
Deadman's Hill
Caroline the Unhappy Queen

Y

8632145

RUSSELL, E.
Return of the
Swastika.

1/-

LONDON BOROUGH OF LEWISHAM
LIBRARY SERVICE

Author

Title

Downham Library
Moors...
Teleph...
Ansafo...
hours

0 7091 0339 01 07

0 7091 0339 01 07

Books or discs must be returned on or before the last date stamped on label or on card in book pocket. Books or discs can be renewed by telephone, letter or personal call unless required by another reader. After library hours use the Ansafone Service (01-698 7347). For hours of opening and charges see notices at the above branch, but note that all lending departments close at 1 pm on Wednesday and all libraries are closed on Sundays, Good Friday, Christmas Day, Bank Holidays and Saturdays prior to Bank Holidays.

03. APR 78
08. MAR 79
17. APR 80
27. APR 82
08. DEC 83
JAN 84
-2. 1986

Downham Library,
... Road, Downham, BR1 5EP
Telephone 01-698 ...
Ansafone Service after
hours - 01-698 7347

Return of the Swastika?

LORD RUSSELL OF LIVERPOOL C.B.E. M.C.

Illustrated

ROBERT HALE · LONDON

© Lord Russell of Liverpool 1968
First published in Great Britain 1968

SBN 7091 0339 5

Robert Hale Limited
63 Old Brompton Road
London S.W.7

LEWISHAM LIBRARY SERVICE

	BRANCH	COPY
LBN.		
SBN. 709103395	07	
CLASS NUMBER 320	CATEGORY	
BOOK-SELLER	INVOICE DATE	
ACC. NUMBER 863215		

320. 14.2.69

PRINTED AND BOUND IN GREAT BRITAIN BY C. TINLING AND CO. LTD.,
LIVERPOOL, LONDON AND PRESCOT

This book is dedicated to the youth of Germany
in whose hands the future lies

Contents

Illustrations

Preface

IT SHOULD not be inferred from the title I chose for this book that I am suggesting that the comparatively young democracy in Germany is about to crack up and that a new Hitler will soon turn the clock back thirty-five years. What I have tried to show is that there have been signs, ever since the early days of the Allied occupation, that the spirit which brought Hitler to power in 1933 is still very much alive and that there is good reason not to be too optimistic about the future. In his farewell message addressed to the German Officer Corps from his headquarters in Flensburg in 1945, Grand-Admiral Dönitz said, "Despite today's complete military breakdown our people are unlike the Germany of 1918. They have not yet been split asunder. Whether we want to create another form of National Socialism, or whether we conform to the life imposed upon us by the enemy, we should make sure that the unity given to us by National Socialism is maintained under all circumstances . . . We must not resign ourselves, that would be the worst thing we could do because it would accomplish nothing . . . Let us use all our strength for Germany."

By 1949 a new "stab in the back" legend had been set on foot by General Halder, and today, although in its early days there seemed little likelihood of it, most of the Bundeswehr are solidly behind von Thadden and his N.P.D. For the first time those who have all along had a real nostalgia for the twelve short but terrible years of the Hitler régime, and those who have no memories of them but are becoming disillusioned with the new democracy can find a common meeting place in the ranks of a political party which has not only already had considerable success at the polls, but which is going from strength to strength and gaining the support of many young people.

The inherent danger of this does not appear to be realized outside Germany except, not unnaturally, by her Eastern neighbours. There are still too many in the Federal Republic itself who do not recognize it or, for one reason or another, wish to play it down. It is for them that this warning is intended, and to the younger generation that this book is dedicated. It is to be hoped that they will see the red light before it is too late, because it is more dangerous to ignore the signs of this new resurgence of German nationalism than it is to exaggerate them.

Acknowledgements

I WISH to express my thanks to the following for supplying me with useful information from their cuttings, pamphlets and books:

The Director of the Wiener Library; the Editor of Gamma Publications; the Institute of Human Relations, New York; the Commission on International Affairs, American Jewish Congress, New York; the Association of Jewish Communities, East Berlin; the Editor of *The New York Times*; Miss Gitta Sereny; the Editor of *Der Spiegel*; the Editor of the *Frankfürter Rundschau*; the Editor of the *Süddeutsche Zeitung*; the Editor of *The Times*; the Editor of the *Daily Express*; Mr. T. H. Tetens; the Wesleyan University Connecticut, U.S.A.; Professor Kurt P. Tamber, the author of *Beyond Eagle and Swastika*; the Editor of *The Cambridge Journal*; Pan Jan Zaborowski, the author of *Dr. Hans Globke the Good Clerk*; Jewish Chronicle Publications; Miss Elizabeth Thompson; Mr. Drew Middleton; Mr. Charles Thayer and the American Jewish Committee, New York.

Also to Mr. Ivor Montagu for allowing me to quote extensively from his article describing an N.P.D. meeting held in a typical German Bierhalle in Harburg in November 1966.

As usual my thanks are due to my wife for the ungrateful task of typing out the manuscript and for much other help and advice during the writing of this book.

Glossary

of organizations and political parties mentioned in this book

B.H.E.	Bundheimattreuer Deutscher (the Refugee Party).
Bruderschaft	the "Brotherhood", a semi-secret society of high-ranking ex-officers.
Bund Nationaler Studenten	youth organization run on the lines of Hitler-Jugend (Hitler Youth)
C.D.U.	Christian-Democratic Union.
C.S.U.	initials used to denote the C.D.U. in Bavaria.
D.A.V.	Deutsche Aufbauvereinigung
D.B.	Der Deutsche Block
D.N.V.P.	Deutsch-Nationale Volks-Partei
D.P.	Deutsche Partei
D.R.P.	Deutsche Rechts-Partei 1946–59 (German Right Party)
D.R.P.	Deutsche Reichs-Partei
D.S.B.	Deutscher Soldaten Bund (German Soldiers' League)
D.S.P.	Deutsche Soziale Partei (German Socialist Party) Berlin splinter group of S.R.P.
D.U.	Deutsche Union (German Union), a radical right-wing organization.
D.V.P.	Deutsche Vaterländische Partei
F.D.P.	Free Democratic Party

G.U.D.	Gemeinschaft Unhabhänginger Deutscher (Association of Independent Germans)
N.R.	Nationale Rechte
N.P.D.	Nationaldemokratische Partei (National Democratic Party of Federal German Republic)
N.S.D.A.P.	Nationalsozialistische Deutsche Arbeiter Partei (National Socialist German Workers' Party), Nazi Party
S.D.P.	Social Democrats
S.R.P.	Sozialistische Reichs-Partei
Stahlhelm	The "Steel Helmet". Revival of ex-serviceman's organization first formed after World War I.
V.D.S.	Verband Deutscher Soldaten-Bund (League of German Soldiers)
V.R.	Vereinigte Rechte (United Right), formed of the federation of D.R.P. and N.R.
W.A.V.	Wirtschaftliche Aufbauvereinigung (Reconstruction Party)

Introduction

On November 11th 1918, an Armistice was signed by the Western Allies and Germany which brought World War I to an end. The German army had suffered a great military defeat, the Kaiser had abdicated and fled to Holland. It was not unreasonable to think, as many people did, that at last the aggressive spirit of Germany which had been the scourge of Europe since its unification under Bismarck, had been laid low and would never be able to rise again. But they were mistaken, and not for the last time.

The internal situation in Germany was one of unrest, and it was within the bounds of possibility that the Bolshevik revolution might repeat itself in the German Reich. Because of this danger, Fritz Ebert, then German Chancellor and a Social Democrat, came to an understanding with the German Officer Corps and this ensured the Army's co-operation in the fight against Bolshevism. And so it was that on December 11th, precisely one month after the signing of the Armistice the returned German Army, with colours flying and bands playing, marched triumphantly into Berlin and up the Unter den Linden. There at the Brandenburger Tor they were welcomed by the German Chancellor with these words: "I salute you who return unvanquished from the field of battle."

Thus was born the legend of the stab in the back: then, in the womb of history, was conceived World War II.

The occupation of Germany had by that time begun, but it was only a very partial occupation and it had one very great disadvantage. Many Americans and Englishmen visited the British Zone of Occupation during those years but few of them, or, indeed, few of the Army of Occupation itself ever went beyond the Rhineland. This created the impression that all

Germans were like the Rhinelanders. Now that is a very false impression. The Rhinelanders are a very different breed of Germans from the people of Prussia to which the Rhineland was forcibly annexed in 1815. Moreover, at that time, the Rhinelanders were on their best behaviour. The remainder of Germany, however, was not under occupation and there was a sovereign German Government in Berlin. In Berlin there was, also, the Control Commission whose duty it was to carry out the disarmament provisions of the Treaty of Versailles.

What possible chance could it have? Every obstacle was put in its way and the disarmament of Germany was never in fact completed. Germany never disarmed, never had the intention of disarming, and for seven years did everything in her power to deceive and counter-control the Commission appointed to control disarmament.

To those who knew these facts it must have come as a surprise to hear Mr. Dulles, the United States Secretary of State, join with Mr. Molotov, the Soviet Foreign Minister, during the famous Berlin Conference some years ago in calling the Versailles Treaty iniquitous. It had, Mr. Dulles said, "been marked by a spirit of vengeance and hatred", and Germany "was the victim of humilitating discriminations and restrictions". The Treaty of Versailles, he said, "had bred war". The Versailles Treaty may have been imperfect, but the Germans could hardly argue that it was unfair. Indeed it was not the Treaty which led to World War II but the fact that many of its provisions were never carried out. In 1918, when it became apparent that Germany would lose the war, a Swiss statesman asked a well-known German diplomat in Berne what sort of treatment Germany expected to get from the Allies if she lost the war, having regard to the atrocities that had been committed by the German Army in France and Belgium. Quick as lightning came the reply, "We shall organize sympathy!"—and organize sympathy they did.

First, they represented the partial occupation of Germany as an "intolerable servitude". They were completely undeterred from so doing by the fact that after the Franco-Prussian War they themselves had occupied some of the fairest provinces of France until the French had paid in full the three billion francs of reparations imposed upon them (£150 million or about 750 million dollars). Secondly they made great play of the misery caused in Germany by the Allied blockade. Thirdly, they complained of what they called the "black shame" of quartering French coloured troops on the Rhine. Fourthly, and this has a familiar ring in more recent times, they held up the spectre of Communism as a dreadful warning to Western Europe.

Furthermore, as happened after World War II, there was in 1919 no general sense of war guilt in Germany. It is true that there was not the same reason for it as there was in 1946 though this should not mislead anyone into thinking that there was none. In December 1914 a distinguished committee, under the chairmanship of Viscount Bryce, was appointed by the British Prime Minister to investigate the alleged outrages committed by the German troops in Belgium and France during the opening months of the war. In its report the committee stated that these allegations were fully established by the evidence and that "murder, lust and pillage prevailed over many parts of Belgium on a scale unparalleled in any war between civilized nations during the last three centuries . . . both in Belgium and France innocent civilians, both men and women were murdered in large numbers, women violated and children murdered". Civilians, including women and children, had been used as a shield for German troops exposed to fire, prisoners of war had been shot and there had been frequent abuses of the Red Cross and the white flag.

Such was the background of the Allied occupation after World War I, and in less than fifteen years Hitler came to power. When Field-Marshal von Hindenburg suddenly and unexpectedly made him Chancellor in 1933 the reaction of the German High Command and the German Officer Corps was not enthusiastic. Nevertheless, though at first critical and even hostile, they subsequently became his sycophants and the acquiescent instruments of their Führer's tyranny and villainy.

For the first three years, however, Hitler was more or less on sufferance, and the Army would have abandoned him without the slightest compunction had it thought that this would have served its own interests. The turning point came, however, in 1936 when something happened which changed the whole picture—the reoccupation by Germany of the demilitarized zone of the Rhineland. Hitler had been secretly planning this coup for months, but when the German General Staff learned of these plans early in the year they were greatly alarmed. They felt certain that such rash action would inevitably lead to a war for which they were not yet ready.

But Hitler knew the Allies better than did his generals. Despite the latter's protests the German forces marched into the Rhineland while Hitler made one of his fiery speeches in the Reichstag. Nevertheless Hitler had some misgivings about the wisdom of this coup. According to his interpreter, Paul Schmidt, he said that the forty-eight hours after the march into the Rhineland were the most nerve-racking in his whole life. "If the French had marched into the Rhineland then we should have had to retreat with ignominy for we had not the military resources at our disposal for even a feeble resistance."

Nothing happened—the Allies offered no resistance. Had they made even a show of force the German troops would have had to retire ignominiously, and that would probably have been the end of Adolf Hitler. But it was not: it was but the beginning. From then on the German generals became mere military yes-men and as the International Military Tribunal said of them in its judgment at the trial of major German war criminals in Nuremberg, "They actively participated in all Hitler's crimes, or sat silent and acquiescent, witnessing the commission of crimes on a scale larger and more shocking than the world has ever had the misfortune to know".

For six years from 1939 to 1945 the shadow of the swastika lay over the occupied territories of Europe like a thundercloud. Hitler had let loose his underworld on Europe and by May 1945 more than five million Jews had been exterminated and several million other innocent victims massacred, the total being probably little less than twelve million. Thus, in less than twenty-one years from her complete defeat in 1918 Germany had been allowed to make a comeback and, once again, to bring death and destruction to her neighbours.

At the end of World War II it really seemed that the hopes of Europe for nearly a century would, at long last, be achieved and the aggressive spirit of German militarism laid to rest. All the armed forces of Germany had become prisoners of war. The German General Staff and the Officer Corps, for the second time within a little more than a quarter of a century, were officially dissolved and their reconstitution forbidden. The Germans were also forbidden to reform any military organization. The dismantling of Germany's war potential, or such of it as had survived the Allied bombing, had already begun and war criminals were being brought to trial.

Never did the prospects seem so bright, but it was not long before the scene changed. Apprehension of Soviet aggression caused a transformation within a far shorter period than was the case after World War I. The rearmament of Germany began in 1954 not under the counter, however, as was done by General von Seeckt by secret contravention of the Versailles Treaty provisions against rearmament, but with the consent and approbation of Germany's former enemies. What is more the new Bundeswehr was formed against the wishes of some Germans themselves who saw, better than many outside Germany, the possible dangers which, in certain circumstances, this might bring about.

There is no point in discussing at the present time, whether the rearmament of Germany was, in the circumstances necessary. Such a discussion is now purely academic and serves no useful purpose. There are many who believe that it was necessary, there are many others who believe, no less sincerely, that it was not. There can be few, however, who are unaware of its risks and dangers. Much more important today than the question of whether or not it was necessary to allow Germany to rearm is this: what is going to happen when her rearmament has proceeded so far that the German Federal Republic feels that she has something to offer to the East and nothing more to gain from the West?

Those who decided to rearm Germany assumed two things.

(1) That the mere decision to rearm her would make the Russians see sense over the question of the reunification of Germany and agree to it upon Western terms.

(2) That after the new German Army had been re-formed, trained and equipped Germany would permanently remain within N.A.T.O.

There seems to have been no real foundation for the first assumption and very little for the second. The Russians are determined not to let a strong reunified Germany once again attack them and for this reason they will never agree to the reunification of Germany save on their own terms, one of which is that Germany should leave N.A.T.O.

The Soviet rulers are in no hurry; a century or two is nothing to them. The policy of Peter the Great is still their policy today. They believe in the "inevitability of gradualness" and they have come to the conclusion that if the German rulers of the future are unable to obtain reunification through alliance with the West they will reorientate their foreign policy and make a deal with the East. They have some reason for this optimism for they have understood better than we have what the ultimate objective of Germany's foreign policy would be should the German Army find its way back into politics.

Before the unconditional surrender of Germany a document was drawn up bearing the signature of Chief of Staff Keitel and Grand Admiral Dönitz, Hitler's political heir, setting out a master plan with two objectives:

(1) To exploit the appeasement plan of the West.

(2) Later, to follow the long term policy of "close co-operation with the East. The "final come back", the document stated, could only be achieved in close co-operation with the Soviet Union. . .

This was the policy laid down by Hitler's successor a few days before the end of the war. The "exploitation" of the appeasement plan of the West was carried out with great success during the fifteen years immediately after Germany's unconditional surrender and has resulted in her becoming rehabilitated, re-armed and extremely prosperous. Furthermore, the view that the future of Germany can be secured only by close co-operation with the Soviets is shared by many of the leaders of political thought in Germany today and there is a foundation in history for this belief. The political and ideological concept that Germany must ally herself with the East against the West is a very old and deeply rooted tradition in German foreign policy dating from 1762, when the King of Prussia faced almost certain defeat at the end of the Seven Years' War. An unforseen event saved Prussia from destruction. The death of the Russian Empress Elizabeth brought Peter II to the throne, and the new Tzar, who was a fanatical admirer of Frederick the Great ordered his armies, which had already occupied Berlin, to leave the European coalition and fight at the side of Prussia. This decision laid the foundations of a Russo-Prussian alliance which ended in the first partition of Poland.

The second important milestone in Russo-Prussian relations took place in 1812 after Napoleon's defeat. The Commander of the Prussian Corps in Napoleon's army, General Yorck von Wartenburg, on his own initiative and disregarding the orders of his King, negotiated a pact with the Russians behind Napoleon's back in the hour of his defeat and brought about the Neutrality Pact of Tauroggen which was the foundation of a second Russo-Prussian alliance and which was to set the seal on Napoleon's fate three years later.

The spirit of Tauroggen, as it is called, has never lost its attraction for the German Officer Corps and throughout the second half of the nineteenth century friendship with Russia was the dominating factor in Bismarck's foreign policy—until it was changed by the young Kaiser and its fruits wiped out by World War I.

It became the guiding theme of the policy makers of the Weimar Republic, Reichswehr Minister General von Seeckt and Count Brockdorff-Rantzau, the first Foreign Minister of the Republic who later became the German Ambassador in Moscow. The idea of a rapprochement with Soviet Russia came up immediately after the signing of the Treaty of Versailles and it is not surprising that it originated in the minds of the Prussian Militarists. The Treaty of Versailles prohibited the Reichswehr from having any armoured units or air force. German officers, by a new arrangement with Russia, were allowed to train at the armoured weapons school at Kazan in Russia where they received the training of which they later made use in Hitler's army. This was brought about by the famous Rapallo Agreement of 1922 which was cemented in April 1926 when the German-Soviet Treaty of Neutrality and Non-aggression was signed in Berlin. This treaty was the forerunner of the Hitler-Stalin Pact of August 23rd 1939, which seems to have taken France and England by surprise. If the lessons of history had only been learned and remembered the surprise might not have been so great.

Moreover, if only the Allied Powers had paid attention to what the Nazis themselves had been saying and writing they might have been forewarned. Something of this kind had been in the Nazi's minds for some time and they had made no secret about it. A few years before World War II Goebbels had said that the day would come when Nazism and Communism would fight side by side against the decadent powers of the West, and the Nazi Party Manual of 1933 advocated that the best way out of Germany's untenable strategic position was through a close tie with Russia.

And what were Hitler's views about a possible alliance with Russia? Rauschning in his book *Hitler Speaks* has recorded these words spoken to him by the Führer in 1934. "Why should I not conclude a pact with Russia when by so doing I can improve our position? The alliance with Russia will be the last trump card in my hand but we must not show our hand too early." It will be remembered that months of secret diplomatic negotiations preceded the Berlin-Moscow Pact which left Hitler free to invade Poland without the risk of Russian intervention. It is quite unthinkable that history might, once again, repeat itself?

The question is when, if ever, and whether there is anything that can be done to prevent it.

Several years ago in an admirable article in *The Times* the following passage appeared:

> Visitors to Germany are sometimes shocked to find Germans inclined to judge their link with the West primarily for its value as a means to serve the end of national unity. They are wrong to be shocked.
>
> Most Governments when they enter an alliance have convinced their people that it is not merely congenial but will serve the national interest. When Dr. Adenauer set out to recommend the Paris Agreement* to his people there were many real advantages to which he could point, but in the end the debate always returned to the one subject, because reunification outweighs in emotional content all other German national aspirations. The majority in Western Germany accepted the Treaties on Dr. Adenauer's word that they were the instruments by which Germany could be united. Western policy at Geneva is the logical sequel. The West could have found no policy more certain of West German support at this stage. But it has to be remembered that the Germans accept it in the hope that it will accelerate a solution of the German

*Signed by the former Allies in 1952 when the European Defence Community was set up, including Germany and designed to lead to her re-armament.

problem. If it were to have the alternative effect of merely postponing a security settlement without bringing German unity any nearer, then it can be argued, and indeed it is, that this is better than nothing for the Germans, since at least it preserves their bargaining power intact. But this is at best a negative gain for them, *and at some stage they may have to consider afresh the use they are to make of their bargaining power.*

There is still today only one political question in the Federal German Republic on which there is almost complete unanimity, and that is reunification, which can only be brought about within the foreseable future in one of two ways—by attacking Russia or with Russian agreement. The Germans know that the first alternative is out of the question and the second is the only practical one.

When Russia was trying to persuade West Germany not to ratify the Paris Agreement Dr. Adenauer said this: "What we are seeking is the association of the free nations of the West because we are convinced that only then can profitable and reasonable negotiations be begun with Russia for reunifying our country. Anyone who believes that *in her present state powerless and tied*, Germany can carry on successful negotiations with the Soviet Union has no eye for the realities of politics. Such a policy would quickly put Germany in the same state of slavery as Russia's other satellites."

Those who read these words will ask themselves the question, what will Germany do when no longer powerless but fully re-armed if she does not obtain from her alliance with the West what she wants from the East. It would be unwise to imagine that the rulers of Germany would not, at any particular time, do what they think is in the best interests of their country or that they would think twice before dropping their present friends if they should appear to have outlived their usefulness. Nor is it wise to assume that by any means all German politicians are good Europeans first and good Germans second.

This is a question which only time can answer and what the answer will be greatly depends on the political events in the Federal German Republic during the next few years. At the present time the Federal German Republic is a full and loyal member of N.A.T.O., and it is, therefore, important that the other members of this organization should do all in their power to support the present democratic régime for should it break down history will surely repeat itself.

Mr. George Brown, the British Foreign Secretary, said in 1967 just before he left London for a visit to Moscow that history "is often a bad teacher", and that there was no possibility of a revival of Nazism in West Germany and that its political leaders were convinced and genuine democrats. That remains to be seen and it is too soon to be so certain. It is true to say that history does not always repeat itself. Nevertheless, German history has done so more than once and it would be foolish and dangerous to ignore this fact.

The future of the Federal German Republic is in the hands of the younger generation, those who are today not more than thirty years old. There are many in Britain today who cannot but look back on our attitude towards Hitler's Germany before the war with anything but regret. We could have done so much to help those who "held up their heads above the crowd" and warned us of what was coming, but we did nothing. Had we only listened to Winston Churchill millions of lives might have been saved. Let us not make the same mistake again by refusing to recognize the possibility of a revival of Nazism.

CHAPTER ONE

The Years of Occupation

TO ANYONE who visited Germany a few months after the Allies began their occupation it was surprising to find the inhabitants looking so well. One had been led to believe that they were all starving but it was only in some of the larger cities that the children looked rather pale and undernourished. There was, however, no comparison with the inhabitants of the territories which had been occupied by the Germans for more than five years.

One was reminded of what one had seen at the end of World War I in the Rhineland where the visible results of the British blockade were nothing to what one had seen when marching through France and Belgium immediately after their evacuation by the German troops. A senior British officer described it in these words: "The Belgians were yellow with hunger. As for the French I shall never forget the look of misery on the faces of the women and children as we passed through Avesnes; the women were gaunt spectres and the children listless little skeletons with skins like parchment. The moment we crossed the frontier with Germany, near Malmedy, I noticed that everyone looked well fed and well clad, the children looking particularly rosy and well nourished."

But for the United States' efforts, while she was still neutral, under the aegis of the Hoover Commission, the Belgian civil Community would have been exterminated by hunger. As a former American Ambassador, Walter Page, wrote in his *Life and Letters*: "Our Belgian Commission is spending more than 100 million dollars a year to keep the Belgians alive."

For anyone who knew these facts it was not pleasant to recall the speech made by the German plenipotentiary, Herr Brockdorff-Rantzau, at the historic ceremony of the signature of the Treaty of Peace in the Hall of Mirrors at Versailles when he ranted against the "inhumanity of the Allied blockade", for a pamphlet had been published in Germany during the war entitled, "*Die Aushungerung Englands*" (The starving out of England), in which its author looked forward with gusto to that country being reduced to starvation by the German submarines.

As they had done in 1919 the Germans were once again blaming it all on the Allies and condemning the mass bombing of their largest industrial centres as a contravention of the laws and usages of war, as laid down in the Geneva Convention, unmindful of the fact that it was they who had begun it. It was also impossible, even then, to meet anyone who would admit to having been a supporter of the Nazi regime, let alone a member of the Nazi Party (N.S.D.A.P.). They all professed to have no knowledge of what went on in the concentration camps or of Hitler's Final Solution of the Jewish Question, the euphemism used for the extermination of European Jewry. Hitler, they all said, and many of them are still saying it, had given Germany full employment and constructed the autobahns and his only mistake had been to lose the war.

It is, of course, untrue that the Germans knew nothing of what went on in these camps. It is equally untrue to say that they knew everything. But there is abundant evidence that a large number of Germans knew a great deal of what went on and that there were still more who had grave suspicions and, perhaps, even misgivings but who preferred to lull their consciences by remaining in ignorance.

As the shortage of labour grew more acute it became the policy to free German women criminals and asocial elements from the concentration camps to work in German factories. It is difficult to believe that such women told no one of their experiences. In these factories the forewomen were German civilians in contact with the internees and able to speak to them. Forewomen from Auschwitz who subsequently went to the Siemen's sub-factory at Ravensbrück had formerly been workers at Siemen's in Berlin. They met women they had known in Berlin and told them what they had seen in Auschwitz. Is it reasonable to suppose that these stories were never repeated? Germans who during the war indulged in careless talk used to be told—"You had better be careful or you'll go up the chimney". To what could that refer but the concentration camp crematoriums?

The concentration camp system had been in existence in Germany for several years before the war and many Germans had had friends and relations confined in the camps, some of whom were subsequently released.

From Buchenwald prisoners went out daily to work in Weimar, Erfurt and Jena. They left in the morning and came back at night. During the day they mixed with the civilian population at work. Did they never converse, and if they did, was the subject of concentration camps always studiously avoided? In many factories where parties from concentration camps worked the technicians were not members of the armed forces and the foremen were not S.S. men. They went home every night after supervising the work of the prisoners all day. Did they never discuss with their relatives or friends when they got home what they had seen and heard during the day?

And what of the S.S. executive staff and guards. It is true that they had all signed statements binding themselves never to reveal to anyone outside the concentration camp service anything which they had seen inside the camps. But is it reasonable to believe that none of them was human enough to break that understanding? The bully is ever a braggart.

In August 1941 the Bishop of Limburg wrote to the Reich Ministries of the Interior and Justice, and of Church Affairs as follows:

> About eight kilometres from Limburg in the little town on Hadamar . . . is an institute where euthanasia has been systematically practised for months. Several times a week buses arrive in Hadamar with a considerable number of such victims . . . The children call each other names and say, "There comes the murder bus again" . . . "You are crazy, you will be sent to the baking ovens in Hadamar". Those who do not want to marry say, "Marry? never! Bring children into the world so that they can be put into the pressure steamer?" You hear the old folk say, "Don't send me to the State hospital. After the feeble minded have been finished off, the next useless eaters whose turn it will be are the old people . . ."

If the local inhabitants knew so much in Hadamar is there any doubt that the inhabitants of Bergen, Dachau, Struthof and

Birkenau knew something of what was happening at their very door in the Belsen, Dachau, Natzweiler, and Auschwitz concentration camps?

The Commandant of Auschwitz, Rudolf Höss himself said of Auschwitz, "The foul and nauseating stench from the continuous burning of bodies permeated the entire area and all the people living in the surrounding communities knew that exterminations were going on at the concentration camp."

Day after day train loads of victims travelled in cattle trucks over the whole railway system of the Reich on their way to extermination centres. They were seen by hundreds of railway workers who knew whence they had come and whither they were going.

Whatever horrors remained hidden behind the camp walls such things as these went on in broad daylight and all those Germans who had eyes to see and ears to hear can have been in little doubt of what crimes were being committed in their name throughout the land.

It is perhaps not surprising having regard to the above that the trials of war criminals did not attract much attention and many of the spectators who attended them did not appear to be horrified by the evidence which they heard at these trials although some of them did. Having had much to do with the trial of German war criminals after World War II I am sometimes questioned about the propriety of bringing them to trial and have often been told it was quite inequitable that such trials should have been conducted by the victors. Although the British and Commonwealth Military Courts conducted their trials with the utmost fairness, and justice was, undoubtedly, done it could be argued that it was not seen to be done, and it is unfortunate that a proposal made some years ago that in future wars the jurisdiction in respect of war crimes should rest with some organization like the United Nations and the trials conducted by independent international tribunals received little support and now appears unlikely to be implemented.

Nevertheless, whether it is right for the victors to try enemy war criminals after their defeat must surely depend on their own record in such matters. Can the victors come to Court with clean hands? It would be folly to suppose that occasionally things were not done in hot blood by the Allied troops which, technically, could amount to a war crime. If an enemy puts up his hands to surrender just as someone is rushing at him in the course of a bayonet charge it may well be quite impossible to avoid killing him, but the doctrine of hot pursuit would appear to take care of that. But those were not the kind of war crimes for which the Allies tried the German war criminals. They were brought to trial for widespread ill-treatment and brutality towards prisoners of war and for killing millions of innocent civilians.

In spite of this the war crime trials have always been resented by many Germans and not only for the reason that they were conducted by the victors, for the German trials which have been taking place in Frankfurt am Main since about 1960 and are still going on have also been severely criticized in many quarters. Indeed this revealing criticism of them appears in the Manifesto of the National Democratic Party of Germany (N.P.D.). "The service of arms is the service of honour . . . while the fathers are publicly stigmatized as criminals with impunity the sons cannot be good soldiers."

It will be seen from the above description of the attitude of a majority of Germans towards the Third Reich and the terrible crimes committed under Hitler's orders that during the first five years of the Allied occupation there was reason to fear that in the new Germany there might, one day, be a revival of Nazism although most of the Allied powers preferred to disregard it.

The reason for this has been well described by Kurt Tauber in his book *Beyond the Eagle and Swastika.** When the Germans were defeated and surrendered unconditionally no one had any idea how long the occupation would last although some Americans were thinking in terms of, perhaps, one or two generations. It was the first time, Tauber wrote, that victors had taken such full responsibility for the vanquished. The occupation was not to be a purely military one until full reparations had been paid. The Allies had made themselves responsible for the "soul of the German people" and for their "moral education and political tutelage".

It was a tremendous undertaking and to carry it out successfully a long occupation was essential and the greatest mistake,

*Kurt P. Tauber, *Beyond the Eagle and the Swastika*, 2 vols. 1967.

from that point of view, was to bring the occupation to an end so quickly, rearm the Germans and incorporate the Federal Republic into N.A.T.O. To do so was, without doubt, a calculated risk and it is still too soon to be able to say with any certainty whether it was worth while.

There was, however, one thing which all the occupying powers realized had to be done, namely, to get rid of all the dangerous Nazis and try to ensure that they should never in the future be in a position to take any active part in the education, administration or government of their country. The necessity for this had been emphasized in the Yalta and Potsdam agreements which had stated that one of the main objects of the occupation must be "the political purification of Germany".

The denazification programme, however, proved in practice to be very little short of a farce. It also operated most unfairly for there were Nazis and Nazis: some had been extremely active and would remain a danger if it were not made impossible for them; others had been merely card-members of the N.S.D.A.P. and had no option of remaining outside the Party because they happened to hold some minor clerical post in government administration. The former were able to engage competent lawyers to represent them when their cases came before one of the tribunals. They also had the advantage of having contacts with important people with false testimonials.

Another serious mistake was made early in 1946 by the Americans in their Zone when they handed over denazification to the *Lander** governments with the obvious result. Apart from this there were other discrepancies in the operation of denazification in the different zones, of which the following are two striking examples.

A former S.S. General, who had been a National Socialist councillor in Berlin heard that the city's tribunal had rejected his claim of restitution for having been removed from his post and interned, said, "Had I known how the Berlin Spruchkammer would decide I would have gone to West Germany after I returned from internment in Russia, for there I would long ago have been reinstated in the public service and paid compensation".

*The government of the various *Länder* (provinces) in the Federal Republic of Germany.

Another leading Nazi wrote the following letter to one of his friends in 1952:

> You'll laugh when I tell you that my first denazification hearing will take place in Hanover next week. For one and a half years I succeeded in postponing these hearings in a race against time, and I was triumphant when the Law for the Discontinuation of Denazification in Lower Saxony was passed before my case came up. Only afterwards did I hear I would lose all my rights from my former public service (such as pension rights) if I were *not* denazified. Thereupon I requested a hearing, getting in just before the dead line. In the written proceedings I have been placed in Group III (Lesser Offenders) with all the prohibitions which go with that. My personal files must have shown all too clearly that I furthered the National Socialist cause materially . . . Everything depends now on getting into Group IV (Followers) without prohibitions and thus obtaining my pension rights.

The above are not the only examples which could be given to illustrate the inequality, discrepancies and abortiveness of the denazification programme. One of the reasons for this was undoubtedly the one given by Charles Thayer in his book, *The Unquiet Germans.*

> By 1946 American officials began to realize that the enemy was indeed not defeated Germany but victorious Russia and abruptly changed their policy. Thenceforth the Germans were to be treated not as outcasts but as a potential ally . . . The Allies based their actions on what Morgenthau had termed "the illogical assumption that kindness will stimulate the rise of a real German democracy committed to a peaceful policy.

In any event by the end of 1949 this change of policy was already beginning to have certain effects which were described in the following leading article in the *New York Times* of December 2nd 1949. It was entitled, "Renazification".

> "The Germans are being scrutinized these days with eyes that are far from tender. The survival of Nazism, the persistence and even the growth of Nationalism, Militarism, and 'Cartellism' are all proving worrisome. The Germans never had democracy in our sense of the word. Their background is one of divided kingdoms and principalities, all under various degrees of autocracy until 1870, when the unification brought a strong, central militaristic Government. The first timid efforts at democracy of the Weimar Republic were soon smothered in Nazi totalitarianism. To expect

German democracy now or in the immediate future is to court certain disappointment. What we have a right to ask is that the effort be made and that some leeway be given in time and opportunity to the teachings and processes that could eventually bring democracy. The problem of getting rid of Nazis (as apart from the far more important issues of getting rid of Nazism or Fascism) is concededly difficult for the occupying authorities. In Italy we succeeded fairly well by making a difference between harmless and bad Fascists. There always was an indistinct dividing line and some bad ones got across. That has also happened in Germany. The quarrel is not that an official, a publisher or a teacher was a Nazi, as it is that some still in office or at work were convinced Nazi-racists, nationalists, believers in totalitarianism. If that element is making a comeback, we have not only lost Germany for democracy: we have lost the war, despite our military victory . . . The United States Commissioner John McCloy said yesterday that there has been 'some rise' in nationalistic tendencies in Western Germany but perhaps not more than could be expected. That was a philosophical way of putting it. Up to a point we must expect a recrudescence and survival of nationalism and even Nazism. The game will not be lost unless the exponents of these theories get control or win a decisive following."

This was written eighteen years ago. The neo-Nazis and those who would quite happily go with them have not yet got control or won a decisive following. Nevertheless, the tide, since then, has not receded and it continues to rise.

This leading article in the *New York Times* was inspired by the reports and articles received from their correspondent in Germany, Drew Middleton, dealing with the not surprising renazification in Bavaria, and one of these articles began with a statement made, as Mr. Middleton hastened to point out, not by a Communist agitator or an excitable tourist but in a report prepared for the Office of the Land Commissioner for Bavaria by one of his chief subordinates. The statement was as follows: "It is very important to recognize that renazification has left Bavaria largely in the hands of those who controlled it under Hitler." This revival in Bavaria was not surprising for it could rightly be called the birthplace of Nazism, but there were already disturbing signs in some of the other *Lander*. The danger of this resurgence of Nazism, as will be recognized by anyone who is in touch with Germany today, is that although the members of the various political parties and organizations which are responsible for it are old Nazis, or so-called neo-Nazis, they are obtaining wherever there is an election, increasing support from many others who either do not care for any democratic government or are disillusioned with the present one.

In Bavaria, however, as the *New York Times* reported, the re-employment in the Government service of former active Nazis was more general and more open than elsewhere and was taking place with State approval. It was this approval which led one of the members of the Bavarian State Assembly, who was never a Nazi, to protest. "Today," he said, "we who were against Nazism and its philosophy are accused of being Nazis. The former Nazis are back in their positions and we are the public fools." To which the State Finance Minister, Herr Klauss, replied, "As Minister responsible for the Bavarian officials I guarantee that we have not accepted *real** Nazis into the administration".

This was, of course, the typical prevaricating statement which Ministers in so many countries are in the habit of making when embarrassing matters are raised in parliament, for the facts were, as the *New York Times* pointed out, that when Herr Klauss made his denial, out of a total of 20,682 civil servants who had belonged to the N.S.D.A.P. or to parties affiliated to it, no less than 14,443 of them "had been dismissed from party activities and later re-instated". Whether any of them were real Nazis or not cannot be proved and Herr Klauss did not, of course, give any definition, but the whole object of "denazifying" in the first place was so that they could not be employed again in government service.

That this had happened in Bavaria showed that denazification had been a complete failure and one of the reasons for this failure was given in a report issued by the Control Commission in the American Zone of Occupation of which Bavaria was a part. The relevant part of this report was published in one of Mr. Drew Middleton's articles. The Denazification Tribunals were frequently understaffed which led to a number of its decisions being "inconsistent with the spirit, and even the letter of the Law for Liberation". Amongst other things this Law

*The italics are mine.

stated that "all those who have actively supported the Nationalist Socialist tyranny or are guilty of having violated the principles of justice and humanity or of having selfishly exploited the conditions thus created shall be excluded from influence in public, economic and cultural life." Nevertheless, according to the report a large number of active Nazis were wrongly classified* as followers, which meant they had only held minor appointments in the Nazi hierarchy, whereas they should have been included in Class I or III which were reserved for those who had held responsible positions.

But it was even worse than that for as early as 1949 in Bavaria it became almost impossible for a *non*-Nazi to obtain an appointment in any government department and preference was nearly always given to former active Nazis many of whom had been officially classified as such.

Some of the statistics given in the *New York Times* were very significant and should have left no doubt in the minds of the responsible Allied authorities in the American Zone that all was not well: for example, more than 20 per cent of the burgomasters in Bavaria were by December 1949 persons who had been proved to have been active Nazis which showed how untrue was Herr Klauss's assurance that "no real Nazis had been accepted into the Bavarian administration."

It was not only the administration that was to such a large extent controlled by former Nazis. The Press in Bavaria, as Mr. Drew Middleton testified, also "showed a Nazi trend" and "more than ninety newspapers were, in 1949, owned and edited by the same men" who had done so during the Third Reich. These newspapers made a point of giving prominence to any criticisms made publicly either in Germany or abroad of the policy or administration of the various High Commissioners in the four Allied Zones of Occupation.

Nor was it surprising that the British were more strongly criticised than any other Western Power, particularly for their dismantling of the war-like industries situated in the Ruhr, which was later unfortunately, and many think foolishly, discontinued, and all were blamed for the division of Germany into two separate States, East and West.

Meanwhile there were other and more ominous signs that the

*One example of this has been given in this chapter.

growing nostalgia for Hitler's Germany was now beginning to come more and more into the open after the formation of three radical right-wing organizations in the British and American Zones. These were the German Union (Deutsche Union), the German Right Party (Deutsche Rechts Partei) and the Association of Independent Germans (Gemeinschaft Unhabhanginger Deutsche). These three political organizations were the first to achieve any prominence and although they were of small dimensions there was always the possibility that they might decide to amalgamate in which event they would be likely to attract recruits from a large section of Germans who for varying reasons were already dedicated to prevent Goethe's "other Germany" establishing itself. During the next two years many other political groups and parties were also formed, the most formidable of which was the Socialist Reich Party (S.R.P.) and it was the first to gain a substantial number of votes at the Lower Saxony elections in May 1951, where, only six years after the ignominious end of the Third Reich, the party won sixteen seats and obtained 11 per cent of the votes, which was remarkable having regard to the fact that ten years after World War I and a mere five years before he came to power Hitler only obtained 3 per cent of the votes cast at the elections for the Reichstag.

This striking success obtained by the S.R.P. in Lower Saxony is probably explained by the fact that this *Land* was one of the poorest in West Germany, and contained a large proportion of refugees from East Germany. It was and is largely agricultural and the party received its greatest support from the farmers and peasants. Another reason for its success may well have been due to the fact that under Hitler Lower Saxony had been extremely prosperous and had received preferential treatment. This prosperity had continued after Germany's defeat in 1945 when food in the cities and large towns was scarce and the *Lands* did extremely well bartering food for jewellery, furniture and clothing. This new-found prosperity, however, had declined when the German currency was revalued in 1948, and this slump in their fortunes made them turn with enthusiasm to the newly formed S.R.P. as they put the blame for the influx of foreign food into Germany, consequent upon the new rates of exchange, fairly and squarely on the Bonn government and, in particular, the more conservative elements of the Government the Christian-Democratic Union (C.D.U.) and the Free Democratic Party (F.D.P.).

The most alarming feature about the S.R.P., however, was the fact that its leaders were all unrepentant Nazis. Otto Remer, the chairman, whose speeches reminded his audiences of the Führer himself, was said by the now defunct British magazine *Picture Post* to have been "the noise of the S.R.P. but not its brain."

On July 20th 1944, the day of the abortive plot on Hitler's life Otto Remer was in command of a crack regiment of guards, stationed at Doberitz, when he received a telephone call from the Berlin Commandant, General von Hase, to hold his troops in readiness for an emergency and to report immediately to Command Headquarters. On his arrival he was briefed on the part his regiment was to play in operation "Valkyrie"* which was to cordon off all the Ministries of the Reich and to prevent any minister or general from leaving the area. On return to Doberitz Remer gave the order for his battalion to march on Berlin and while he was doing so one of his officers Lieutenant Hagen, a dedicated Nazi, told him that he had just seen a car pass in which Field Marshal von Brauchitsch was sitting in full uniform†. This made him suspect that a military *putsch* was in progress and he suggested that Remer should check with Goebbels who was the Gauleiter of Berlin. Remer was not himself a convinced Nazi but he was naturally anxious to be on the winning side of any military *putsch*. As soon as possible he got in touch with Goebbels who told him that Hitler was still very much alive and that he would broadcast to the nation later that evening. Before the broadcast, however, the Führer, at Goebbel's suggestion, spoke to Remer personally on the telephone and told him to place himself under the orders of Himmler whom he had appointed Commander-in-Chief of the Home Army. From that moment Remer swung right round, paraded his troops and delivered a patriotic speech which, when Goebbels informed his Führer, earned for Remer immediate promotion to the rank of Colonel and the task of capturing the

*See *The Nemesis of Power* by John Wheeler-Bennett.

†In fact it was not von Brauchitsch who was sitting in the car. Hagen had mistaken his identity.

conspirators. He was awarded the 'Ritterkreus with brilliants' for his part in suppressing the *putsch* and was subsequently appointed Major-General.

It is important, having regard to the fact that Otto Remer became leader of the S.R.P. less than five years after all this happened, to remember what the position was immediately after Germany's unconditional surrender. Her defeat was complete and the entire armed forces became prisoners of war. The sovereignty of Germany ceased to exist and passed into the hands of the Occupying Powers.

The German Officer Corps at the moment of their country's defeat awaited a final exhortation from the man who had succeeded Hitler, Grand Admiral Dönitz. They did not have to wait long, and Dönitz's farewell message, in the words of John Wheeler-Bennett, was "full of that spirit of vibrant resilience which had sustained the Officer Corps in past defeats".* The counsel which Dönitz gave them was similar to that which their predecessors had received from von Schleicher in 1918 when he told them to return to their homes and wait upon the order of events but not to resign themselves to acceptance of the prevailing reversal of their fortunes.†

Within a few years, in 1949 to be exact, General Halder was publishing it abroad that had it not been for Hitler's personal interference in the conduct of military affairs the German High Command, even had it not succeeded in winning the war, would have avoided the completeness of the defeat. This time, the "Stab in the Back" had not been struck by the Social Democrats, as in 1918, but by the military incompetence of the Führer and the inefficiency of the Nazi regime. Very soon after this, however, a second stab in the back was put round by those who wanted to perpetuate the Hitler myth. According to them it was the anti-Nazi element in the German army which had been responsible for the July 20th *Putsch* which had stabbed Hitler in the back and prevented him from bringing the war to a successful conclusion.

It was significant, therefore, that it was this legend which was incorporated by Remer into the propaganda of the S.R.P. and

**Op. cit.*

†The text of this farewell address was found in his desk at Flensburg though there is no evidence that it was ever delivered publicly.

fostered by Count Westarp who was the brains of the party and had the distinction of being prosecuted and convicted for having falsified his denazification questionnaire.

Events were, very soon after the formation of the S.R.P., to play into the hands of the militarists owing to the fear of Soviet aggression and within a few months of the decisions made by the Western Powers in New York and Brussels in September and December 1950 regarding the necessity for re-arming Germany several ex-servicemen's organizations came into being and nine months later most of them became affiliated with the newly formed Deutscher Soldaten Bund (the German Soldiers' League—D.S.B.). It was these events which led to the questions with which John Wheeler-Bennett ended the Epilogue to his book which was published in 1953. "Will the D.S.B. become a political lobby for the demands of the military upon the Bonn Government? Or will it confine its activities to the care of those ex-servicemen and their dependants who are not absorbed into the new Wehrmacht? Within the answers to these questions lies the solution to the mystery which is the source of so much apprehension attendant upon even partial German rearmament. Is there a new spirit abroad in Germany or is this merely 'where we came in' in the repetitive history of the German Army in politics?"

This last question still remains to be answered. There are, so far, no signs that the German Armed Forces have any influence over German politics but since the rise of the N.P.D. began certain things have happened which would seem to make it unwise to state categorically that the repetitive history of the German Army in politics is dead and buried once and for all.

One of the Vice-Chairmen of the N.P.D., Herr Gutmann, has stated that "at least 1,200 Bundeswehr soldiers from raw recruits to active colonels" are members of the party. That is only a small percentage, but there is reason to think that in future elections the N.P.D. is likely to obtain much greater support from the armed forces.

A captain in the German Air Force named Wolfgang Ross, the son of a former S.S. officer was given leave from his unit just before the *Land* elections in Bavaria at which the N.P.D. met with such success, so that he could stand as a candidate. He conducted his campaign and was duly elected and given his discharge. This took place at a ceremonial parade attended by the whole of the 4th Army Air Force Battalion in which Ross was a Squadron Commander. The Commanding officer read out the retirement order signed by the Federal Minister of Defence, Herr Schroder which commended him for his faithful service to the German people and the entire battalion was given the day off after the parade had been dismissed.

After leaving the Air Force when interviewed by *Der Spiegel*, Herr Ross stated that 25 per cent of the Bundeswehr would vote for the N.P.D. and that it ran through all the ranks. What the men in the forces liked about the N.P.D. was that instead of telling them their service was for democracy they were told that military service is "a service of honour for the Fatherland".

Another leading figure in the N.P.D. was Dr. Fritz Dorls who joined the N.S.D.A.P. in 1929 but was later expelled from it. This was to serve him well when denazification was being carried out by the Allies after the war and he was allowed to join the staff of a Christian Democrat paper. When, eventually, after being elected in 1949 a member of the Bonn Parliament as a German Reich Party (D.R.P.) candidate, he was soon expelled from that party, he then founded the S.R.P.

In a pamphlet entitled *Germany's New Nazis*, published in 1951 by the "Anglo-Jewish Association" in London, the following comment on the S.R.P. appeared:

> In spite of its completely undemocratic structure, however, it will be interesting to see if it too, will be able to digest Dr. Dorls's peculiar qualities. An interesting aspect of this gentleman's activities is that his name is frequently mentioned in connection with charges of co-operation between the Socialist Reich Party and the East Zone Communists. If, as seems quite probable, these charges have a basis in fact, it is beyond doubt that Dr. Dorls is behind the intrigue.

Among Dr. Dorls's observations on contemporary politics the following is outstanding both for style and content: "The German people do not need democracy and do not want democracy. They must be led and they want to be led." Whether or not the Socialist Reich Party were willing to go all the way with Dr. Dorls in respect of that declaration it certainly has the backing of past German history.

The majority of the members of the S.R.P. were between the

ages of 20 and 40 and were almost entirely males, and both Remer and Dorls proudly boasted that it was primarily the party of youth. About 30-60 per cent of them, varying according to the geographical situation, were expellees and refugees. Another interesting sidelight was that the large majority of its members were of the Protestant faith in the same way that in the late nineteen-twenties, to quote Mr. Kurt Tauber,* "the heavily Catholic areas proved largely impervious to the blandishments of radical socialism".

By November 1951 it was becoming evident that the S.R.P. was daily gaining support, particularly in Northern Germany, and the Federal Government instructed the Bundesverfassensgericht (the Federal Constitutional Court) to institute proceedings against it. During the previous few months some of its leaders appeared to be eager that the party should be put to this test, for they believed that its electoral successes had been so widespread that Bonn would not dare to court unpopularity by taking such a step, and that if such proceedings were instituted there would not be sufficient evidence to justify a judgment against them.

On January 1st 1952, however, raids were made on the party's Headquarters and on the homes of some of their leaders where much valuable evidence was discovered in the files and private correspondence; but even then there was considerable optimism within the party where it was thought unlikely that the proceedings would be brought to a conclusion before the federal elections which were to take place in 1953. This optimism, however, proved to be misguided for the Constitutional Court, realizing this possibility, closed the last line of escape by giving an interim judgment, in the form of an injunction prohibiting the S.R.P. until such time as the Court was ready to give its final judgment, from carrying on political activities of any kind whatsoever.

On October 23rd 1952 the judgment of the court was given and they found the S.R.P. "subversive to the Constitution". They declared that "it should be dissolved and that no substitute organizations should be formed". All its property was confiscated and all its members who held seats in the Federal and State parliaments or local government bodies were deprived

*See page 31.

of them. "The most palpable Nazi threat to the Young Republic has ended in a fizzle, discredited even in the eyes of the extremists themselves, Bonn had given unmistakable notice to the world at large, but more importantly to the radicals within its own borders, that it would not permit Weimar history to repeat itself. This lesson did not fail to make its impact on the thinking of the more moderate National Opposition".*

There is, however, another lesson which this must surely give to "the world at large" unless it is too blind to see the wood from the trees. A democracy which can only survive by outlawing its opposition must be inherently weak, and it is this undoubted fact which makes it impossible at this early stage to say, with any certitude, that the new Germany has come to stay.

Be that as it may; it is no wonder that as early as 1951 while the Allies were still in occupation of Germany, many people were already asking themselves whether post-war Germany would become a really democratic State or whether it would go back to Nazism or aggressive militarism. The American Jewish Committee in September 1951 published the first of a series of reports on the growth of neo-Nazism in Europe which stated that the problem posed by the S.R.P. and "its hard core of cohorts" was aggravated by the evident willingness of the other more respectable parties to seek votes on much the same extreme nationalist elements in other parties including some which had representatives in the Bonn coalition government, and this was corroborated by the U.S. High Commissioner for Germany at that time Mr. John J. McCloy in the 9th Quarterly Report on Germany issued in February 1952. "Unhappily, most of the established political parties have also been stocking the merchandise of nationalism. Individuals or circles . . . have expressed highly nationalist sentiments either out of conviction or as a vote getting device. Even some Federal Ministers have not been above such actions." Whether these nationalist sentiments were expressed because of conviction was comparatively unimportant. The fact that they gained many votes and were used for that purpose was of far greater significance for it clearly demonstrated that there were still many people who regretted the passing of the Third Reich.

*Kurt P. Tauber, *Beyond Eagle and Swastika.*

The American Jewish Committee, asked what was being done about these neo-Nazis and the question was particularly relevant at the time because the West German Government had been talking about banning the S.R.P. but had so far taken no legal steps to do so. All it had done was to announce that a Bill was being drafted which would require all political parties to disclose the sources of their financial backing.

One experienced writer on German affairs, who was quoted in the American report, stated that a comparison of the period from 1919 to 1924 with that of 1946 to 1951 revealed such uncanny parallels that many a person without blindly believing that history repeats itself in identical fashion could not help projecting certain trends five or ten years into the future. He pointed out, for example, that even as late as 1928 the Nazis had secured only 3.5 per cent of the vote while the conservative element, the Deutsche Nationalische Volks Partei secured 14 per cent, yet within five years the roles were reversed. The Nazis had gained 44 per cent and the conservative percentage had dropped to only 8. This showed what great changes could take place in a very short time.

But what was important in the eyes of the American Jewish Committee was what many others were thinking, namely, that it was not the size of these German nationalist organizations which was important, but their viability. Experience of the past few years immediately following the beginning of the occupation had shown that "post-war nationalism grafted on to previous growths" had found a favourable political climate in Germany, and that when the right moment came it could suddenly expand and seize power. The U.S. High Commissioner was in full agreement with this conclusion of the American Jewish Committee for the following statement appeared in his 1952 report: "The danger on the extreme right is not of a critical nature and —at least in the form of the S.R.P.—does not constitute an immediate danger to the Federal Republic, but there *is a potential danger* whose nature and importance warrant continued vigilance by all who value democratic principles." That can be said today with the same truth as in 1952 and, indeed, with even more justification.

The disbandment of the S.R.P., however, was not the end of neo-Nazi and nationalist re-awakening in Germany. During the next twelve months there were many other indications that the Germans were not becoming any less receptive to a new and, in some cases, a somewhat disguised representation of the same old Nazi gospel. In addition to the S.R.P. between 1949 and 1953 there were as many as 317 other extreme Right and Nationalist groups of varying size and importance in the Federal Republic. Many of them were of little importance and attracted little support but the sum total of their significance was considerable.

The German Socialist Party (D.S.P.) was a Berlin splinter of the S.R.P. and had very few members. The main plank in the platform of the Refugee Party was, of course, a demand that the former German territories east of the Oder-Neisse line should be returned. The Reconstruction Party (W.A.V.) which was only permitted to exist in the American Zone of Occupation had considerable success in Bavaria and in 1949 won twelve seats in the Federal elections. Its leader was Alfred Loritz, a Bavarian lawyer, who had a varied and strange background. During the last two years before Hitler's accession to power he was actively anti-Nazi both as a journalist and as chairman of the electoral district of Oberayen/Schwaben, and when Hitler came to power he joined the underground Resistance movement and remained with it until 1939 when he had to flee to France. The following year he was tried in his absence by a People's Court and sentenced to death. On returning to Munich after the war he resumed his practice as a lawyer and, almost at once, formed the Wirtschaftliche Aufbauvereinigung (W.A.V.). The party met with some success during the Bavarian *Land* elections, in 1946, most of its support coming from expellees and refugees. About the same time Loritz became the Bavarian Minister for Denazification.

However he soon ran into serious trouble and in May 1947 became the subject of an inquiry set up by the U.S. Military Government and the Ministry of Denazification. The inquiry found that Loritz had used his official position to further his party's ends, and some of the party's funds were thought to have been provided by a number of wealthy defendants who had, in this way, obtained lenient treatment when they appeared before a denazification tribunal.

Since 1939, however, his political attitude had changed, and back in Bavaria he saw the possibility of obtaining political power and boasted that if he did he would "institute a system not like Hitler's but like Himmler's" under which he would "exterminate" all his political enemies. While Loritz was at one and the same time Minister of Denazification and leader of the W.A.V. he admitted a large number of what were technically known as "lesser Nazis" into the party which began to develop a strong Nazi flavour and he also succeeded in persuading a young man, 27-years-old, Karl Meissner, to join it. Meissner had previously held a minor official post with the Free Democrats, and was a fiery demagogic orator, and Loritz immediately put him in charge of the W.A.V.'s propaganda department, but this did not last very long and in 1947 Loritz expelled Meissner from the party. Meissner immediately founded a new party, Der Deutsche Block (D.B.), and tried to get a licence for it from the U.S. authorities, but without success. Nevertheless he was able to form a D.B. splinter group in the Bavarian Landtag consisting of five out of the thirteen W.A.V. members.

Although the policy of the D.B. was originally a moderate one, it was not long before it became outwardly more like the N.S.D.A.P. than any other party in Germany. Meissner's public meetings became more and more like the old Nazi rallies. They included torch parades, the playing of Hitler's favourite marches and when Meissner appeared on the platform, the audiences raised their hands in the Hitler salute and shouted "Heil". The stewards at every meeting were dressed in uniform shirts with the famous armbands and all wore jackboots and the evening always ended in violent brawls with Left Wing opponents who tried to break up the meetings.

By the end of 1949 the speeches of Meissner were strongly reminiscent of the Führer's. At a meeting in Memmingen in December Meissner spoke as follows:

> A large part of the democratic values are lies . . . Behind the conceptions of freedom, which the occupation authorities have been preaching to us since 1945, stand the Morgenthaus, Baruchs, Frankfurters and Lippmans . . . The German people have learned to know what Bolshevism is as no other people have. Of course the advance and retreat of the German Army could be experienced only by German soldiers, not by concentration-camp inmates . . . The "Iron Chancellor", Bismarck, has become a "Rubber

> Chancellor", Adenauer . . . The German Bloc [D.B.] is fundamentally in favour of a German Army as a matter of national education. The youth must again learn discipline and order. The ideas of Communism, Marxism and liberalism are coming to an end. Something brand new has to be created . . . Any improvement, however, can only come when the present system has been destroyed! The democracy of today no longer has a raison d'etre, because it has failed. Parliamentarianism has outlived its usefulness . . . Instead we need a state structure with disciplined leadership and order.

All this was allowed to go on apparently without any interference by the U.S. Military Government although the Left Wing parties did their best to break up these meetings determined, as they publicly announced, that "history would not repeat itself and that Munich must never become once again the capital of a Nazi Regime".

The attitude of the French occupation authorities was much more realistic. France, unlike Great Britain and the United States, had suffered five years of Nazi occupation and knew their Germans better. For this reason all nationalistic activity in the French Zone was strictly forbidden, and Meissner or anyone like him would have been subject to immediate arrest had he crossed the border between the French and American Zones. Nevertheless, the French Zone was to become the home of an entirely different nationalist revival operated by what has been described as "the erstwhile Social revolutionary-so-called Left Wing of the Conservative Revolution, with all its tendencies towards sect-like, utopian, Christian communism and national Bolshevism," a peculiar kind of mixed grill, in which former members of the Black Front played a prominent role, the foremost of whom was Otto Strasser who with his brother Gregor had been leaders of what was generally known as the socialist wing of the N.S.D.A.P. As early as 1930 Otto had a violent disagreement with Hitler and resigned from the party and formed the Black Front. This organization though it gained only moderate support was regarded by Hitler with the greatest suspicion and those of its leading members who were unable to get out of Germany quick enough were sent to concentration camps within a few days of Hitler becoming Chancellor. Otto Strasser, who received warning from his brother that this was going to happen, managed to cross the frontier into Austria in the nick of time and eventually found asylum in Canada. Immediately after Germany's defeat, Strasser, still in Nova Scotia, regained contact with a number of his old colleagues, after their liberation from the concentration camps, and in July 1950 the League of Germany's Revival was founded with Strasser as nominal chairman although he still remained in Canada. Strasser's League received very little support and the main reason for this was undoubtedly because it was not pro-Nazi and had, therefore, little attraction for the majority of discontented Germans.

Of the other extreme Right and Nationalist groups which came into being during the first five years of the Allied occupation the following were the most notable*:

German Socialist Party (D.S.P.)

This was an affiliated branch of the S.R.P. and had its headquarters in West Berlin. Although its leader Aberhard Stern protested that he had never been a member of the N.S.D.A.P. the D.S.P. was outwardly, at any rate, more Nazi than the S.R.P. itself and when its offices were raided in 1951 party uniforms and swastika flags were found in large quantities. Strangely enough during the same raid documents were discovered which disclosed the fact that the party was in contact with Communists in East Berlin.

German Reich Party (D.R.P.)

Like the S.R.P. this party received most of its support in Lower Saxony (Niedersachsen). Shortly after five of its members were elected to Bonn in 1949 two of them joined the S.R.P. In the forefront of its policy was the "primary goal of reunification", the re-establishment of a Deutsches Reich with frontiers "determined by historic right and the will of the people", an end to discrimination against former Nazis and the reappointment of government officials who had been "illegally removed from office" by the denazification measures. By 1949 it was already a dying force and in the federal elections it obtained no more than 5 per cent of the votes cast. It eventually merged with the N.R. and the two federated parties were subsequently known as the United Right (Vereinigte Rechte, V.R.).

*See *Germany's New Nazis*—Jewish Chronicle Publications, 1951.

THE BROTHERHOOD (BRUDERSCHAFT)

This was a semi-secret society of high ranking ex-officers.

THE STEEL HELMET (STALHLHELM)

This was a revival of an ex-servicemen's organization first formed after World War I but it is entirely different and should not be confused with such organizations as the British Legion and Les Anciens Combattants. Its primary objective was never the same and it was used from the outset to persuade the Allies of the necessity of rearming Germany. The original Stalhlhelm when Hitler came to power in 1933 co-operated with the S.A. and it would do much the same thing again should the opportunity ever arise.

THE LEAGUE OF GERMAN SOLDIERS (VERBAND DEUTSCHER SOLDATEN-BUND, V.D.S.)

This organization, like the Stalhlhelm, as might be supposed from its name, existed for the sole purposes of looking after the welfare of ex-servicemen, but it became a source of disquiet early in 1951 when its leaders began to involve it in politics. It was in that year that a large number of mass rallies were held all over Germany at which high-ranking officers made inflammatory speeches. The first of these took place at Kassel, and was presided over by the former commander of the famous Grossdeutschland Armoured Division, General Manteuffel. In his speech he said that there could be no co-operation between Germany and N.A.T.O. until all German ex-Generals then serving sentences for the commission of war crimes had been released and denazification had been discontinued.

At another rally former General Ramcke called for the German soldier to be cleared of all guilt and he included in this demand ex-members of the S.S., the S.D., and the Gestapo. It is not surprising, therefore, that the Bonn correspondent of the *Observer*, in 1951 reported that the League was regarded by many German democrats as "being in danger of becoming a tool for the political ambitions of a limited number of professional officers".

It was apparent, therefore, as early as 1951 that already, and at a time when Germany was still occupied by the victorious Allies, the spirit of the Third Reich was still very much alive. This realization was confirmed by a series of public opinion polls which were taken by the U.S. High Commissioner's Office during the early part of 1951, dealing with the following subjects:

(1) The opinions of Germans as to whether Nazism was good or bad.
(2) The attitude of the Germans to the question of war guilt.
(3) The number of Germans who would resist the return of a Nazi régime.
(4) The strength of anti-Semitism in West Germany.

In answer to the question, "What would be your attitude in case a Nazi party or one like it should come to power in Germany," only 20 per cent said they would do everything to prevent it; 13 per cent said they would like to see it happen, or would give such a movement their support; 2.3 per cent said they would not care; and 30 per cent said that although they would not like to see it happen they would do nothing to prevent it; 14 per cent expressed no opinion being, doubtless, uncertain whether or not their replies to the questionnaire would be kept confidential.

When the U.S. Commissioner announced these figures he was addressing a meeting of students at Freiburg University in January 1952, and said, "It is alarming that so great a proportion of the German population is disinterested in the political structure of the country . . . Too few Germans show themselves disposed to oppose extremist political movements."

With regard to the Germans' attitude towards war guilt the question asked was as follows:

> Assume that three Germans are talking about the war and about everything Germany did during the Third Reich; with whom of these three would you agree?
>
> Herr Muller says, "Each German bears a guilt for Germany's actions during the period of the Third Reich; and everyone should acknowledge this guilt."
>
> Herr Schmidt says, "Not every German needs to feel guilty, but each one should feel the responsibility to rectify, in so far as possible, the wrongs which Germany committed during the Third Reich."
>
> Herr Schultz says, "Germans in general need feel neither guilt nor responsibility for rectifying any wrongs. Only those who committed crimes are guilty as well as responsible."

The replies were as follows: only 4 per cent agreed with Herr Muller, which was not unreasonable as there is no justification for the principle of collective guilt; 21 per cent agreed with Herr Schmidt and 12 per cent either had no opinion or gave no answer, but *63 per cent thought that "Germans in general need feel neither guilt nor responsibility for rectifying any wrongs"*.

The German attitude to the Jewish question at this time was not so positive doubtless because in 1951 there were only 15,000 living in Western Germany. In one of these public opinion polls the following question was asked: "Would you prefer that the Jews still living in Germany should remain and make their homes here, or would you prefer them to emigrate." Of those who were asked this question 37 per cent stated that they did not care either way, and 10 per cent had no opinion. Of the remaining 53 per cent, those who wanted the Jews to go and those who wanted them to stay were almost equal in number.

It would seem, therefore, that by the middle of 1952 there was already a large number of extreme Nationalist parties and organizations many of them varying to a considerable extent in their neo-Nazi element, and although the judgment of the Constitutional Court in Karlsruhe which disbanded the S.R.P. was a setback to the growing revival of Nazi nostalgia it also had the effect of driving the neo-Nazis underground, where they could be equally if not even more dangerous as neo-Nazism began to infiltrate itself into more respectable circles.

One of these was the party known as the Free Democrats (F.D.P.) which was the third largest member of the coalition Bonn government at that time.

Many members of the defunct S.R.P. joined other Nationalist parties such as the Deutsche Partei and the B.H.E. and some of the war veterans organizations. Day by day more Germans, who were not attracted by any of these parties sufficiently to support them openly, continued to harp more than ever on the undoubted fact that Hitler brought a certain amount of prosperity to Germany by curing unemployment and building the autobahns and protested that the "so-called crimes" committed under the Nazi regime had been grossly exaggerated. They also pointed out that Hitler had been right in his determination to overthrow Communism and the ever worsening relations between the

Soviet Union and the Western Powers lent great weight to this argument. Furthermore, many former prominent Nazis were beginning to reappear in the civil service and police forces all over the country; and this was happening not only under the eyes of the Federal Government but in some cases with the approval and support of some of its members.

One of the chief duties of the Minister for the Interior in the Bonn Government, Dr. Robert Lehr, was to see that such men were no longer allowed to be in government employment, yet it was he who appointed many senior S.S. and Gestapo officers to important positions in the Federal police force and, when attention was drawn to this in the Bundestag, he refused to dismiss them from office. This kind of thing, as stated in an article published in the London *Jewish Chronicle*, discouraged many ardent democrats who were actively anti-Nazi during the Third Reich and made them inclined to retire from the political scene. "The growing conviction among many of their opponents", the article stated, "that the State neither can nor will fight for democracy when challenged does in fact represent the Trojan Horse of the new Nazis."

But it was not only Dr. Lehr who refused to dismiss eminent Nazis from government appointments. The Federal Chancellor himself, Dr. Adenauer, set all his Ministers a bad example by refusing to dismiss Dr. Globke whose appointment in the civil service had occasioned severe criticism in Germany itself and in many other European countries. Globke had written the official Nazi commentary on Hitler's Nuremberg Racial Laws which, as Cassandra wrote in the *Daily Mirror* in 1961, "were the basis on which the treatment of the Jews by the Nazis was made legal. They led to the gas ovens of Auschwitz and all the unspeakable abominations of the concentration camps."*

Dr. Adenauer's obstinacy in continuing to allow Globke to hold such an influential post, that of Chief of the Chancellor's Office, has never been satisfactorily explained, and for someone who suffered as he did under Hitler it is incapable of a satisfactory explanation. This is what Herr Gerhard John, a member of the Bundestag, said about Globke as reported in the *Frankfurter Rundschau* on July 19th 1961 shortly after his name was mentioned on the thirty-eight day of the trial of Adolf

*See Chapter IV.

Eichmann in Jerusalem: "He was one of the henchmen of National Socialism who, ignoring the basic tenets of the Weimar constitution, provided legal assistance to the realization of Hitler's insane racialism. Globke was never compelled to give such assistance and cannot account for it. What is essential is that as a commentator of the so-called racial laws, Globke did sully the good name of Germany. That is why from the point of view of the Federal Republic's honour he cannot be supported."

Globke, however, was not the only ex-Nazi who the Chancellor was quite happy to have employed once again in the Foreign Office in Bonn although their records during the time they held office in the same department under Hitler obviously made it most undesirable. Wilhelm Melcher, Dr. Kurt Heinberg and Werner von Bargen were three of them. One of Melcher's assignments during World War II was to organize the activities of the Grand Mufti's fanatical supporters in the Middle East; Heinberg directed the East European Division of the Nazi Foreign Office which co-operated with Himmler's R.S.H.A.* in the massacre of Balkan Jews; and von Bargen, as representative of the Foreign Office in Belgium, was responsible for and took part in the deportation of Jews and members of the Belgian resistance to the concentration and extermination camps.

Another senior civil servant in one of the Ministries in Bonn who had been an active Nazi was Dr. Emil Ehrich, formerly an officer in the S.S. and the N.S.D.A.P.'s head representative in Italy during World War II. There were several protests made at the time of his appointment to the Bonn Administration but, although at first, Adenauer refused to have him dismissed he was eventually forced to give up his post but immediately went to Lower Saxony the cradle of neo-Nazism, second only to Bavaria, and became party organizer for the C.D.U. prior to the elections due to take place in May 1951. That a man with his background should have been chosen for this job is not surprising, and it is evident that it was, at the time, considered to be an advantage, for the fact that he had held the rank of Obersturmbannführer S.S. was advertised on all the C.D.U.'s election posters.

There was no doubt in the minds of those who were stationed

*Reichsicherheitshauptamt, Reich Security Head Office, Himmler's headquarters.

in the British Zone, and especially in Niedersachsen and Westphalia that these May elections were fought, as *The Economist* put it in its issue of May 12th, "on lightly Nationalistic platforms". For some months before the elections the Germans had been getting rather uppish. In nearly all the garrison towns in the Zone, and particularly in the neighbourhood of Bad Oeynhausen where Rhine Army headquarters were situated, leaflets had been pushed under the front doors of those houses that were occupied by the British telling them it was time they went home. British officers and their wives were frequently insulted in the street by passers-by and swastikas were painted on the walls of many houses and buildings occupied by members of the British armed forces and the Control Commission of Germany.*

The number of ex-Nazis who by the end of 1952 had been reinstated in important government appointments was quite large and was increasing every day.† As the well-known German writer Rudolf Pechel stated in an article which appeared in the *Deutsche Rundschau* as early as July 1951, "Our people are still suffering from a spiritual and moral disease. This is shown not merely by the number of Nazis and their fellow travellers who have appeared in official positions, government offices and the press, but by the fact that they are now in a position to carry out the restoration of Nazi ideas as they wish."

The situation a year later, by which time what has often been called the 'restoration'‡ frame of mind had had a considerable effect on German public opinion, was well summarized in a report issued by the American Jewish Committee of New York in July 1953.

*A typical incident which demonstrates the attitude of the German authorities in the spring of 1951, and in which the author was involved, took place at Vlotko on March 31st 1951. The incident itself is described in Appendix II, together with the reactions of the British High Commissioner's office and His Majesty's government towards it which clearly indicated that Noel Coward's famous song, "Don't lets be beastly to the Germans" had become the signature tune of the British and American Occupation authorities.

†Particulars of some of these men will be found in Chapter IV, "Voices from the Past".

‡This looked to a revival of what the Germans considered were their old fashioned virtues, and the re-acceptance of authority (*obrigkeit*) which brought Germany power and prestige in the past.

German public opinion seems to be veering towards more noxious nationalist themes. There is a growing sentiment that Hitlerism held much that was good, that its faults have been exaggerated. The need to build western defences against Communism has been seized by the neo-Nazis as a confirmation of Hitler's foreign policies; the impression spreads that Hitler was right and the Democracies wrong in their approach to world politics. Thus with regard to foreign as well as internal affairs, the tendency to discredit Democracy gains strength. In this climate of opinion the worst elements in Germany have achieved virtually complete success in their campaign to recapture public approval. War criminals, S.S. troopers and former Nazis of similar stripe (*sic*) are again regarded as good Germans who were merely doing their duty . . . in this atmosphere the authors and publicists who helped lay the ground work for acceptance of Hitlerian ideas, such as *Lebensraum*, are back in business . . . Because of the perceptible shift in their approach they influence party programmes without drawing particular attention to themselves. Ideas similar to theirs are becoming common currency. It is against this changing background that the progress of neo-Nazism in West Germany must be measured and its potentials evaluated.

The British exposure of the Naumann Plot in Januray 1953 uncovered many of the activities of the nationalists during the previous five years which had been carried on more or less underground. It was on January 14th that six former prominent Nazis were arrested by the British occupation authorities. They were, Dr. Werner Naumann, Dr. Gustav Schiel, Herr Paul Zimmermann, Dr. Henrich Haselmeyer, Herr Heinz Siepen and Dr. Karl Scharping.

Naumann had been an S.S. Captain and Under Secretary of State in Dr. Goebbels' Ministry of Propaganda and had been nominated in Hitler's will to succeed Goebbels. On May 2nd 1945 he managed to escape from Berlin together with Martin Bormann and, for the next five years, lived under an assumed name and earned his living as a mason's apprentice. He had joined the N.S.D.A.P. in 1928 when he was only 19 years of age. It was not until after the 1950 amnesty declaration that he became manager of the import-export firm of Messrs. Lucht.

Schiel, a former Reich Students' Leader had also been nominated in the Führer's will to take over the post of Reich Minister of Culture and had taken some part in the formation of the Bruderschaft* one of the earliest organizations for the revival of Nazism. When arrested he was working as a physician at a Hamburg clinic.

Zimmermann had been the equivalent of a brigadier in the S.S. and had been appointed in the Economic and Administrative Department of Himmler's R.S.H.A. where his duties mainly consisted of helping to run some of the concentration camps. After the war he had been an adviser to the Iron and Steel Trust where he was closely in touch with many of the important industrialists in the Ruhr and with some of the ex-Nazi advisers who had taken refuge in Cairo.

Haselmeyer had also been one of the early members of the N.S.D.A.P. and took part in the abortive Munich *Putsch* in 1923. As an expert on Hitler's "racial science" he took a leading part in the Nazis' programme for the sterilization of the unfit.

Siepen had also held a number of responsible administrative posts under the Nazi Regime and, at the time of his arrest, was on the board of a steel works in Solingen, while Dr. Scharping had been in the broadcasting department of Goebbels's Ministry of Propaganda.

Within a few hours of the arrest of these six alleged conspirators a seventh was taken into custody. He had been a leading Nazi and for some time was the gauleiter of Hamburg. He was one of the very early members of the N.S.D.A.P., having joined it in 1921, and after Germany's surrender he was detained in an internment camp for three years. Very soon after his release he played an active part in forming the Bruderschaft.

It was not long after Naumann's reappearance as the result of the 1950 amnesty that he came into contact with a man named Achenbach, who happened to be the lawyer employed by the import-export firm of which Naumann was the manager. Achenbach had been Counsellor in the German Embassy in Paris during which time he was responsible for rounding up about 2,000 Jewish hostages in reprisal for the killing of two German officers. As a result of this meeting with Achenbach Naumann decided to try and form what they called an elite cadre of ardent Nazis who felt themselves at a loose end when the Bruderschaft was dissolved. The idea behind this decision was to work slowly, subtly but deliberately for the return of

*See page 49 above.

Nazism to power by gradual infiltration of the major political parties already in existence which were regarded by the Allies as eminently respectable and genuinely in favour of a democratic government in Germany. Naumann and his associates knew that with the Allies in occupation of their country there was no possibility of achieving this by more violent means. They also thought that by working for this end underground they would be unlikely to rouse the suspicion of the occupation authorities.

When the British made these arrests they were acting under the provisions of the Occupation Statute which gave them the power to arrest any German who appeared to be "a threat to the Allied troops", and the British Foreign Secretary, Anthony Eden, made a statement in the House of Commons to the effect that while the information in the British Government's possession was not sufficient to prove that the activities of this small minority of unrepentant Nazis constituted an immediate threat to the democratic order in Germany their potential danger in the future could not be ignored. It was for this reason that it had been decided that this conspiracy should be brought out into the open and thoroughly investigated. It was then the intention of the British Government to hand over the arrested men, together with all the documentary evidence which they could obtain, to the Germans to be dealt with as they thought fit. When that was done Eden announced in Parliament, "the German authorities might decide not to prosecute some of them, in which event they will be released, but their detention, interrogation and the impounding of their documents will have provided valuable evidence for the prosecution of Naumann and his associates".

The German reaction to the action taken by the Control Commission for Germany was extremely hostile, for the Bonn Government, not unnaturally felt more than a little embarrassed at this disclosure, so soon after Germany's defeat, that their new constitutional régime was not so firmly established as some of them were inclined to believe. Perhaps the history of the Weimar Republic was in danger of repeating itself. They protested that the British should have made the evidence available to them before taking such drastic action in which event, they said, they would have been quite capable of dealing with the alleged conspirators on their own. Dr. Adenauer thought it necessary to assure the Allies and the world outside that there was no danger to the democratic government in Germany. "I can assert", he said, "with all the emphasis at my command, that there is no danger whatsoever of a Nazi party, on the Hitler model or any other, being able to seize power in the Federal Republic . . . I am convinced that if a new party representing such a tendency were formed and put forward candidates at the coming election it would end in a resounding fiasco. . . . Nevertheless, the Naumann-group, though numerically small, must be carefully watched."

An excellent summary of the general criticism of the British action, particularly that which appeared in the press, was issued by the Wiener Library of London in July 1953, including reports published in some of the leading London newspapers and in a certain section of the German press including comments which appeared in *The Times*, the *Manchester Guardian*, the *Frankfurter Allgemeine*, the *Neue Zeitung*, the *Tagespiegel* and the *Frankfurter Rundschau*.

One of the ministers of the Bonn Government, Herr Hellwege, criticized the British for having been "badly advised". He thought, and here he betrayed definite Hitler leanings, that a Nazi conspiracy was "far less dangerous to the Federal Republic than the activities of Eastern agents who were backed by unlimited financial resources", and he regretted the fact that the German socialist democrats and the trade unions had applauded the British action.

One of the chief leader writers in the *Frankfurter Allgemeine* complained that the British had "created more neo-Nazis in eight days than Naumann and Siepen have been able to do by the sweat of their brows for years". Other German journalists put the whole thing down to a commercial conspiracy by British industrialists against the firm of which Naumann was manager, and they also suggested that by entrusting the investigation of the conspiracy to the Germans themselves the British had made a "silent confession of failure" and had only done so in order to rid themselves of an accusation which they knew full well they would not be able to justify. Some newspapers frankly refused to believe that there was any substance whatsoever for the allegations and that in any event "the plot was not more than a political tea party".

There was, however, a considerable amount of documentary evidence to support the British action, a great deal of which was published in the *Frankfurter Rundschau* in June 1953 under the heading "The Grave-Diggers are among us", and they established the following facts.

Naumann was in 1950 as ardent a Nazi as he had been in the days when he was very close to Hitler, for he wrote in his diary, "You cannot betray an ideal in which you have believed from your early days as I have done. Maybe the ruins of the Reich Chancellery hold for us greater values than are dreamed of by rash critics". This was probably why he obtained employment in the firm owned by Herr Herbert L. Lucht who had held two important posts under Goebbels, being First Secretary for Cultural Affairs in the Ministry of Propaganda in Berlin and later in a similar department in Occupied France.

It was, however, after he had had a long talk with the Nazi sculptor, Arno Braker, who persuaded him to "get back into politics" that Naumann saw the possibilities of carrying on where he had left off after Hitler's death in 1945. After meeting Braker, Naumann wrote in his diary:

> Of course Braker urged caution but I should not let things drift. He said that of all the people he knew only one was really able to master the situation, and that was I. According to him I was able to put forward ideas which would adopt the good things of the past and add what the new times required. I should withdraw to lonely places and work it all out. He is so convinced that only young new forces can really do it that he advises against Guderian. Such people were merely a handicap. His demands weigh heavily on my mind and I have grave doubts whether I shall be able to fulfil his expectations.

Despite the doubts, however, Naumann took Braker's advice and managed to gain contact with a few of his former Nazi friends and colleagues, and formed them into what he called a Gauleiterkreus, and three months before he and his friends were arrested they held two meetings at which Naumann gave details of his political programme. His plan was gradually to build up a large nationalist opposition throughout Germany by means of infiltrating the parties which already enjoyed considerable support and were at that time outwardly, at any rate, democratic. He was most anxious not to start a new party which would be bound, sooner or later, to meet the same fate as the S.R.P. had done only a few months earlier. "Political leadership Cadres" were to be formed and trained before any appeal was to be made to the masses. Naumann had already seen the fatal results of precipitate action and was determined not to make the same mistake. After all, there was plenty of time; the Allies were still occupying Germany but that was not likely to last much longer. With them out of the way, the right moment would, doubtless, arise by which time the ground would have been properly prepared.

Naumann's fellow conspirator Heinz Siepen described the plan in military terms. The "first wave", i.e. a Nazi revival must be restrained: "short circuit tactics" which have been tried before without success and, indeed, played right into the enemy's hands, must not be repeated. What he called the "second wave" must be the centre and right wing of the political arena and when these had been won over the time would be ripe for the "final assault".

This policy of gradual infiltration had already begun to have some success, before the discovery of the Naumann Plot, in the Deutsche Partei and the B.H.E. (the Refugee Party). The greatest success, however, had been achieved in the F.D.P. In August 1950 Naumann had written in his diary that in order to influence political events the "National Socialists must join the Free Democratic Party, swamp it, and then take over the leadership". He was convinced that a cadre of no more than 200 would be able to take over the party's most important regional branch in Westphalia where almost all the executive posts were already held by former Nazi functionaries. Naumann had paved the way for his intended infiltration of the F.D.P. by getting his great friend, former S.S. Colonel Wolfgang Diewerge, a former high official in the Propaganda Ministry and a fanatical anti-Semite, appointed secretary and political adviser to Dr. Friedrich Middelhauve, then leader of the F.D.P.

In the speech which he made at the meeting in Hamburg of the Gauleiterkreus Naumann explained the details of his infiltration plan. "There should be large organizations" he said, "for the farmers, for the several soldier's associations, for the retail traders, the refugees and the tax payers. We ought to make ourselves heard in the local councils and our men should become

Councillors and Mayors . . . we should infiltrate into all organs of public life and *when they have been sufficiently won over the hour for a united front will have arrived.* This is our aim. Let us work for it tirelessly day by day. Let us close our ranks more tightly than ever, let us form a dedicated fellowship of a few hundred, sworn to keep the faith, and we shall be a power which, though as yet in the background, will one day achieve in the eyes of the world those ideals for which we once were called up and for which our comrades laid down their lives." One thing, however, was of paramount importance and it was the key to the success of the whole plan. For the time being there was to be no conspicuous activity which could only lead to disaster.

Future developments within the F.D.P. during the last three or four years proved that Naumann was quite right when he warned his colleagues that it would be unwise to expect too much from the Free Democrats despite the fact that many of its members and some of its leading men had strong Nazi leanings. There was also quite a strong liberal wing in the party and the disclosure of the Naumann Plot helped these liberals in their constant tussle with the nationalistic members and in April 1953 steps were taken to sever the ties between this nationalistic wing and the Naumann infiltrators who had become an embarrassment. This gave an opportunity for a mild purge of the more extremist elements.

Naumann was, however, extremely optimistic that he would be able to attract considerable support from a large cross-section of the German people who, though they were not really Nazi-minded, were not attracted by the new democracy and who had supported the S.R.P. which many of them thought was the lesser evil. Now that the S.R.P. no longer existed there seemed to Naumann to be an opportunity to get them back into the fold. They were neither organized nor homogeneous and they needed a leader to turn them into a political force in the same way as the Führer had held them together. Naumann said that the bond which had previously held them together ceased to exist after May 1945 and it could only be restored by some other form of authority which so many Germans seem to require.

He was also optimistic enough to believe that the Federal Parliament, like the Weimar Republic, would not last long and he hoped that it would be the last. Nevertheless, he hoped that it would die a natural death and stressed once again that time was needed and that no precipate action should be taken. "There is enough to be done now", he told his committee, "without launching a new party. To prepare the soil, sow and reap, is not possible all in one go. Let us first take care of the soil."

In the course of preparing the soil Naumann had every intention of doing what he called "correcting the current notion of Nazism". He stated that he did not want to go on playing "the old records" because they no longer played accurately. "We are no neo-Fascists", he said, "for the simple reason that the things that once existed are for us a matter of the past . . . we have moved beyond the ideas of Nazidom . . . we need a new style, new conceptions, new slogans, a new language if we want to give our people another political shape. That style must not be emphatic, propagandist, wallowing in superlatives, but strictly matter of fact and serious minded."

Knowing the dedicated Nazi background of Naumann and his clique, therefore, many Germans were tempted to ask the question, "Where exactly do they stand?" "Our position", Naumann told them, "is not where infertile attempts are made to launch parties which at their very best are so feeble that they cannot live to see the first dawn. . . . No doubt many of those associated with these parties"—and here he was doubtless referring to people like Otto-Ernst Remer and Hermann Bernhard Ramcke—"have in the past distinguished themselves by courageous words and personal sacrifice, but having been unable to achieve success because their programme, their leadership and *their timing* had been at fault they now hope to make good by joining forces with others as weak as themselves." There was one thing which Naumann intended at all cost to avoid, namely that what he called "the enemy", at home or abroad should be able to point at Naumann and his followers as a gang of wild extremists who were seeking to plunge Germany into a new undemocratic adventure. The course which Naumann wished to follow, in any event during the early stages, was between Adenauer and Ramcke. "That", he said, "is where the right road lies."

It was in keeping with this extreme caution, which Naumann

was quite sure would pay a handsome dividend, that he did not have a press medium of his own, nor was it necessary for him to have one as he was able to get valuable assistance from two periodicals which were already in existence and were as outspoken as he was tight-lipped. They were the *Deutsche Soldaten Zeitung* and *Nation Europa*. The former was the organ of the D.S.B. (Deutsche Soldaten Bund) which was controlled by former S.S. Colonel Dr. Wilhelm Spenler and edited by Herr A. W. Uhlig. Spenler had been a senior official in Himmler's R.S.H.A. and Ulhig had served under Goebbels in the Ministry of Propaganda, and he could not have had stauncher allies. Both were in touch with the Gauleiterkreus. *Nation Europa* was the monthly journal of the Fascist International whose editor received instructions from Naumann in regard to German affairs, and eventually he obtained a controlling financial interest in the paper with the help of a group of Fascists in France.

The Naumann dossier, some details of which have been given above, showed that Nazi influence and tradition were still alive although still only lurking in the background, and the British High Commissioner, Sir Ivone Kirkpatrick, was justified in saying at a press conference held shortly after the arrest of Naumann and his colleagues that they had been plotting to regain power in Western Germany and that there was *prima facie* evidence that this group was trying to infiltrate supporters into the three established German political parties.

The British Foreign Secretary, Anthony Eden, although he said that the British Government did not consider the Naumann group as an immediate threat to the German régime, stressed the fact that its long-term plans constituted a potential danger. "It is clear", he said, "that these men some of whom were close to Hitler in 1945 regard it as their mission to form a mass movement based on Nazi ideology with a view to capturing political power in Western Germany. Their leader has made it clear that it is his intention that the existing democratic parliamentary system should be brought to an end as soon as feasible. The groups activities are directed to this end. While content to work in secret for the present their immediate purpose is to permeate all branches of society and to seek by degrees to transform certain of the existing parties and/or organizations into National Socialist fighting groups . . . with this purpose in view, they have been planning to establish widespread contacts inside and outside Germany, and have been seeking to place their agents secretly in positions of influence." These words summed up precisely what the Naumann Plot was all about and it was, indeed, fortunate that it was nipped in the bud before it came to fruition.

But there were other signs that not enough ex-Nazis were being prevented from returning to positions in which they would be able to exercise influence and try to sabotage the new democracy. Many thousands of former N.S.D.A.P. members since the defeat of Germany had found their way by 1953 into posts which gave them some sort of connection with the post-war regime and all the three major political parties were competing for their votes and they were, from the party's point of view, wise to do so for from a number of public opinions polls held during those years it was clear that more than 50 per cent of those who felt able to give an answer to the question whether there was "more good than evil in the ideas of Nationalism" were of the opinion that the good exceeded the evil.

The denazification programme kept the top Nazis out of harm's way, but only temporarily, because after their cases had been heard and their dossiers examined they were given a document certifying their denazification. Once they had obtained this "clearance certificate" the way back was not difficult and they were soon able to rehabilitate themselves and return to economic, professional and even political life sometimes, in the eyes of many Germans, with enhanced reputations.

The failure to carry out a thorough reform of the civil service was also a most unfortunate omission and there is overwhelming evidence that as early as 1950 more than 50 per cent of the civil servants in government offices had been Nazis. According to an American report several varieties of former Nazi party members included:

(1) A relatively small group which remained Nazi by conviction who were embittered and completely incorrigible.

(2) A considerably larger group of professional people and technicians who were mainly concerned about their own careers.

(3) A host of nominal or insignificant ex-party members.*

> They are confused by charges which associate Nazi crimes with the traditional German nationalism; they are tempted to justify the war and to blame the Allies for failing to understand that they were really fighting Soviet Russia to defend the West. They confuse war criminals with soldiers performing legitimate military duties. They worry about German honour . . . without being willing to admit that through the Nazis German honour suffered almost irremediable harm.
>
> Often, with perverse logic they lay all the blame on the Nazis, or on Hitler personally, and thus exonerate to their own satisfaction all other Germans from any blame or responsibility for the past. And by the same token they argue that the Allies are the cause of all their present problems and must be responsible for their future. They are, in short, a much perplexed people trying to find their way out of a deeply disturbing and humiliating experience without loss of confidence or self-respect.†

During these years much had been said and done by Germany's leaders to combat anti-Semitism and make the German people realize the enormity of the crimes committed by the Nazis against European Jewry. Carlo Schmidt, deputy leader of the Socialist Democratic Party, said in a speech made to the Bundestag in April 1951 that those who had suffered most under the Nazis hardly dare raise their voices as they met with an almost total lack of comprehension and sympathy, and for that reason alone the case of the Jewish victims called for special consideration. "People", he said, "have a tendency to forget, as they have already forgotten, the anti-Jewish persecutors, the extermination of the Jews in the gas chambers—of all the victims of the Nazi Regime, the Jews suffered the most terrible fate. That is why we have a moral responsibility, especially towards the Jews . . . It is our inevitable duty to do whatever we can for those whom the Nazi criminals chose as their principal victims." But it was Dr. Heuss, the first President of the new republic, who spoke out more strongly about the Jewish persecution than anyone else. The Germans, he said, ought to feel "a collective shame", and he called for a new

*Office of the U.S. High Commissioner for Germany, "The Radical Right". Seventh Quarterly Report on Germany, April-June, 1951, p. 34.

†Office of the U.S. High Commissioner for Germany. *Report on Germany, September 1949-July 1952*, pp. 106-7.

approach to what Hitler had called "The Jewish Question", and at the same time Dr. Adenauer told the Germans that they must repair the wrongs done to the Jews and fight with the utmost energy those forces which had not yet realized that intolerance and arrogance are the grave-diggers of liberty.

These two pronouncements had followed a most important declaration of government policy made in September 1951 which was the forerunner of discussions which took place later with Jewish representatives and the Israeli Government regarding the payment of compensation for the "unheard-of-suffering" to which the Jews were subjected as a result of the Nuremberg Laws and the Final Solution of the Jewish Question. This declaration had stated that "unspeakable crimes were perpetrated in the name of the German people which impose upon them the obligation to make moral and material amends".

While all this was going on, however, a campaign was being carried on in the Federal Republic to reprieve infamous war criminals like Ohlendorf and Pohl who had been tried and sentenced by the Allies. Otto Ohlendorf had been in command of a Special Action Group (Einsatzgruppe D) composed of S.S., S.D. and Gestapo, and other police units attached to Field-Marshal von Manstein's Eleventh Army in Prussia which was responsible for the mass execution of many thousands of Jews by shooting, hanging, gassing, and drowning. Obergruppenführer Oswald Pohl was at one time in command of the S.S. headquarters in Munich which was responsible for the administration of many of the concentration and extermination camps, including Auschwitz where not less than three million people were put to death. The campaign was unsuccessful, but the fact that it took place and received considerable support is evidence that anti-Semitism was still widespread even though it was under the surface. Both these men were duly executed in Landsberg Prison, where the major war criminals convicted at Nuremberg met their fate, but the Bruderschaft and Remer's party called it murder. These were the same men, and they included von Thadden the present leader of the N.D.P., who paid an official visit to the cemetery at Landsberg in memory of the war criminals executed there.

In a report issued by the Foreign Affairs Committee of the Anglo-Jewish Association in 1951 other instances of the persistence of anti-Semitism in Western Germany were given, including some amazing statements which the neo-Nazis were continually making. One former Hauptsturmführer stated on oath that there had only been one concentration camp gas chamber in Germany. That was at Dachau, and it had done a proper job cremating prisoners who had died of old age. An even more extraordinary statement was made by one of Remer's supporters who said that "the Americans had appointed tribunals composed exclusively of Jews to sentence Germans to death".

The S.R.P. warned the Jewish Committee in the British Zone that if they were wise they would support the campaign for the release of the seven Landsberg war criminals who were under sentence of death otherwise they would find another wave of anti-Semitism sweeping Germany as it did in 1933. This was reported in the *Sunday Times* in May 1951. Meanwhile the desecration of Jewish cemeteries continued and on one occasion, which happened to be the anniversary of Hitler's birthday, after the Jewish cemetery in Munster had been desecrated a leaflet was left behind with a swastika printed on it calling on the Germans to rise from their "defeat at the hands of Ahasuerus".* The idea for this leaflet had been taken from an anti-Semitic book of religious stories used in the Catholic schools in North-Rhine-Westphalia. According to a German newspaper, the *Frankfurter Rundschau*, the education authority which had passed the book for use in the schools stated that the word Ahasuerus had been inserted afterwards, and that as soon as this was discovered the book was withdrawn from publication. Nevertheless, the paper stated, one of their correspondents found no difficulty in buying as many copies as he wished several weeks after the book had been banned.

Although these anti-Semitic incidents were not of such a nature as to indicate a general revival of anti-Jewish feeling or resentment they occurred with sufficient frequency to show that it was by no means dead and buried. It was, also, to some extent, reassuring that they were reported and condemned in a number of newspapers. One of these stated in a leading article that there was still no sign of a change of heart in Germany in a sense of a

*In much anti-Semitic literature which was current in Germany during the Third Reich this was the name given to the "Wandering Jew".

complete rejection of all forms of anti-Semitic propaganda, and drew attention in this connection to re-nazification, the failure to purge Nazi elements from public life, the glorification of men who had committed atrocious crimes against humanity, the insufficient protection of Jewish cemeteries, inadequate restitution and an increasing tendency to delay and avoid the payment of compensation to the victims of Nazi persecution.

In the *Neue Zeitung* a non-Jewish German wrote to say that he was shocked to hear the word "Jew" being so often used as a term of abuse. This, he stated, "was symptomatic of the views of certain circles in Germany, to whom the expulsion and torture of several million Jews means nothing more than the death of a netful of fish drawn from the sea, whose agonizing death they could watch without batting an eyelid".

Another sign of the survival of anti-Semitism, mentioned in the Anglo-Jewish Association's pamphlet referred to above, concerned the fact that it was extremely difficult, if not impossible to find a publisher in Germany for any book which told the truth about Hitler. One of these was Count Kurt von Blucher's book, *Know Your Germany* which argued that the whole of Hitler's policy was based on the doctrine of the Master Race and the idea that a non-Aryan could not be a citizen of the Reich and should be "exterminated". Whereas any German general could write his memoirs, whatever his war record was, and there would be no difficulty in finding a publisher. The diary of Anne Frank, however, had tremendous sales due, doubtless, to the fact that it was a dramatically written tragic story which had a universal appeal.

Early in 1953 the Public Affairs Department of the United States High Commissioner's Office announced the results of a public opinion poll conducted in the U.S. Zone in the previous December principally on two questions, the increase in neo-Nazism, and the attitude of the ordinary German with regards to restitution to the Jews. The result of this inquiry, being announced only a fortnight after the arrest of the Naumann plotters, was most unpopular and first and foremost among the critics was Chancellor Adenauer himself, who protested that the figures given would, unfortunately, be misinterpreted.

It is quite certain that they were unlikely to encourage those whose fondest hope was to see the new democracy growing in popularity, though they must have been most welcome to those who still held the view that such a form of government was entirely out of keeping with Germany's history and tradition, for they indicated an increase since the previous survey held in May 1951, only eighteen months previously, of nostalgia for the Third Reich.

The percentage of those who were of the opinion that there was more good than evil in Nazism had risen by 10 per cent and among those who were between the ages of 18 and 24 the percentage was even higher. In answer to the question of whether former Nazis should have the same chance for advancement in business and politics 58 per cent were of the opinion that they should. Asked whether they agreed with the view expressed by General Ramcke that to be a war criminal was an honour, 31 per cent said "Yes", and only 25 per cent definitely disapproved. It was, therefore, somewhat surprising that only 19 per cent agreed with General Remer that those who took part in the unsuccessful attempt to assassinate the Führer on July 20th 1944 should be classed as traitors. The figures with regard to the advisability of rearming Germany, to which a majority of Germans were thought to be opposed, were even more alarming, for 47 per cent voted for a West German national army while 27 per cent said that they would prefer a number of German Divisions integrated as a part of a European Army. A majority, according to the High Commissioner's office report, however, stated that "they would like to see West Germany the strongest country in Western Europe and wanted her to play *the leading role** in the Europe of the future."

Opinion polls can often be misleading but when like is compared with like the conclusions are not far wrong. On this occasion the figures of the 1953 public opinion poll could be set against those published in 1951 and were, therefore, all the more revealing.

The other fact that came to light was the attitude of the West Germans in 1953 towards the Jews and, as the report issued in July of that year by the American Jewish Committee in New York stated, since anti-Jewish agitation was the prime objective of the Nazi regime, the post-war attitude of the Germans towards the Jews could be viewed as a yardstick whereby

*The italics are mine.

German progress towards democratic ideas may be measured. There could, at that time, be no doubt that the average German refused to acknowledge what the Nazis did to the Jews and preferred not merely to ignore the past but even to pretend that it never existed. The neo-Nazis publication *Nation Europa,** frequently contained articles exactly similar to many which during the Third Reich appeared in Streicher's anti-Semitic magazine *Der Sturmer*, and there were many other periodicals which were exactly similar. Perhaps the most sinister of them all was a leading pro-Nazi magazine called *Der Fortschritt* and it was in one of its issues that an article appeared claiming that only a million and a half Jews were exterminated and that the remaining four and a half million were the invention of Germany's enemies.†

Nevertheless, in 1952 the Federal Government had sent a delegation to the Hague where negotiations took place with representatives of the Israeli Government and a number of Jewish organizations which resulted in the following:

(1) "Pay 3,000 million Deutsche Marks to Israel (more than £200 million) to recompensate for the expense of resettling so great a number of uprooted and destitute Jewish refugees from Germany and from territories formerly under German rule . . ."

(2) "Pay the Conference on Jewish Material Claims Against Germany, 450 million Deutsche Marks, (more than £30 million) in order to make available for the rehabilitation of Jewish survivors, part of the heirless assets, and other uncovered funds which had belonged to Jews who had been killed by the Nazis."

(3) "Pass legislation to redress some of the Nazi wrongs and improve the existing legislation for the indemnification of private individuals."

The necessary legislation to ratify the agreements to pay the sums mentioned above was passed through the Bundestag by what would appear at first sight to be a very large majority, but if the votes are looked at carefully it will be seen that although the Socialist Party voted unanimously in favour of the legislation, with the exception of fifteen absentees, there were no less

*See page 63.

†This kind of nonsense does not take place only in Germany. In a review of my book on Nazi war crimes *The Scourge of the Swastika* in which I modestly put the figure at "over 5,000,000" a reviewer stated that the number was only 4,372,000 as though it was possible to estimate the real figure to the nearest thousand.

than forty-five members of the C.S.U. (which is the Bavarian wing of the Christian Democrats), the Free Democrats and the Deutsche Partei who voted against it. It was, also, entirely due to Adenauer's personal hold over the Christian Democrats that no member voted against the measures, but even he was unable to prevent twenty-three of them from abstaining.

Furthermore, there is other evidence that this legislation was not popular with everyone, for a special survey was made by the Officer of Public Affairs of the U.S. High Commissioner in Germany to discover the people's attitude towards paying compensation to the victims of the Nazis. "As you know, the Federal Government is trying to provide for those who suffered damage by the war of the Third Reich. Which of these groups should in your opinion receive such help and which not? If Jews and some other groups should get help, which of these groups would have the greater right in your opinion to get such help? Of those who answered the question 68 per cent said that the Jews should receive *some* help, but only 2 per cent said that they should have top priority; 17 per cent thought that the Jews had the least right of all to receive any compensation while *no less* than 21 per cent said that the Jews should get nothing at all.

When the result of this survey was published the High Commissioner's Office made the following observations in its report. "Half of West German population", it stated, "cannot be counted upon to support restitution measures, and even many of those who were in favour of restitution to Jews revealed that they had anti-Semitic views." Typical of the observations made to the interviewers who conducted the survey, according to the report, were as follows: "They have enough already"; "They look after themselves"; "They have been adequately helped by the various authorities"; "They have exploited us in the past"; "They are foreigners and not our responsibility"; and finally, of course, "I am against the Jews".

Public opinion polls taken over a period of years since then have not been any more encouraging, and in the Manifesto of the N.P.D. the payment of compensation to the Jews is referred to as the "extortion" of millions from the German people.

CHAPTER TWO

First Years of Independence

FROM 1954 until the violent outbreak of anti-Semitism on Christmas Eve, 1959 the new democracy appeared to be making considerable progress towards stability. It really seemed that, at long last, the spirit of German militatism would be laid to rest. But apprehension of Soviet aggression caused a transformation, in a far shorter period than after World War I, and the rearming of Germany began. Even then there was no indication whatsoever that the prospect of serving in the armed forces had any attraction for German youth. The Navy and the Air Force had some attraction for obvious and peaceful reasons but the Army, though greatly changed and a valuable addition to the strength of N.A.T.O., was no longer, as formerly, the ambition of every schoolboy. The military man was no longer placed on a pedestal and a uniform no longer attracted the girls. A young man is not called up for military service until he is twenty-one and then he has only to serve for one year. Most of them, when the Bundeswehr was first formed, accepted service in it as a necessary duty.

The Army itself was unrecognizable as I was to see for myself when I paid a visit to the 4th Panzer Grenadier Brigade at Gottingen, under the command of Brigadier-General Count von Baudissin. Wolf von Baudissin* was a brilliant young officer on Rommel's staff in North Africa. He had been one of the most impressive personalities in the military resistance movement, whose members are regarded by many Germans today as traitors, and he worked unceasingly with his friend Major-General von Tresckow to rouse a group of officers to resist the growing abuse of the Wehrmacht. He helped to plan repeated attempts on Hitler's life. When the final attempt, known as the

*See also Chapter VII.

July Plot, was made on July 20th 1944, von Baudissin was a prisoner of war in Australia, and so he survived.

Fortunately for the Bundeswehr, he was the chief planner of the Army reforms in the Ministry of Defence under Herr Theodor Blank and is largely responsible for the new citizen Army which its predecessors would scarcely recognize. Many of these reforms were so revolutionary that they did not find favour with some of the older officers who had returned to the colours. The new informal uniform, the absence of spit and polish and of the old barrack square drill parades disturbed these old soldiers.

The discipline of the Reichwehr, they argued, produced the greatest army Germany ever had: why change it? This talk of a "democratic" Army was all nonsense. It must be the Prussian system again.

There were other signs at that time which gave grounds for hoping that the new Republic might have come to stay. The old people did not appear to be greatly interested in politics. So much of their world had changed that all most of them wanted was to be allowed to live and die in peace. The majority of the middle-aged group felt uncomfortable for so many of them were compromised by the past. It was largely this which made it difficult to teach the young about Hitler and it explains to some extent why no real attempt was made to do so.

The young people appeared to be quite uninterested in the past and to have shed the German reverence for authority which was responsible for their parents and grandparents co-operating successfully with Imperial Germany, the Weimar Republic, the Third Reich, the Allied occupation and the new Federal Republic. These young people were, however, as pointed out in another chapter, quite indifferent to political life and were inclined to say, "Let the Government go on *ohne mich* (without me)". All this, of course, was before the N.P.D. was even formed.

It was not long, however, before there were definite signs that the Army was changing, for in 1956 the Ministry of Defence issued a regulation permitting the recruitment of former Waffen S.S. personnel in ranks equivalent to those which they had held under Hitler. There was some protest about this but the Bonn Government refused to rescind the regulation and this criticism was lulled by a promise that all former Waffen S.S. who applied to join the Bundeswehr would be carefully screened. Nevertheless, the magazine *Look* stated that "the rebirth of a German army and the return of an officer corps that served Hitler has given impetus to the maintainance of traditional attitudes".

It was very shortly after that a series of anti-Semitic incidents took place which gradually led up to the "return of the Swastika" which is described in detail in Chapter III. The pessimism which this roused amongst many people was well expressed in an interview with Dr. Henrik van Damm which was published in the *New York Post:*

> I try to be realistic. There is a problem but it is not primarily a Jewish problem. It's the problem of democracy in Germany. There has been no real revolution in German thinking, and that's the real pity.
>
> Right after the war they became pacifists. Then they were told to fight in the cold war. "N.A.T.O. needs you", and the Germans once again have begun to think that strength is what counts. The military man has regained status.
>
> The German army is more dangerous internally than externally. The veterans' organizations—all former officers—are the ones protesting against the trials of former Nazis and concentration camp commandants. They openly criticize those who participated in the bomb plot against Hitler. We are seeing the revival of an anti-democratic philosophy which has never disappeared from Germany. It is more dangerous than anti-Semitism, which it usually includes.

This last statement hits the nail right on the head, for it is true to say that Jew baiting in Germany is one of the ways in which the Germans, who are still nostalgic about the Third Reich, can best express their feelings, and anti-Jewish prejudice is traditional and ingrained in Germany. It flourished long before Hitler was ever heard of and it was not only the Left-Wingers who were blamed for having stabbed Germany in the back in 1918. The Jews were also made scapegoats.

A warning light was seen in 1957 when the Zind affair took place. During the war a Jew named Kurt Lieser (he was, in fact, only half Jewish but was classed as non-Aryan under the Nuremberg Laws) had been sent to the concentration camp at Sulz and also had miraculously escaped the gas chamber during the "Final Solution". When the war started he had been living in Offenburg and after the defeat of Germany he very unwisely decided to return there only to discover that he and his family were not accepted by the other inhabitants and were more or less ostracised.

One evening on the way home from work rather later than usual Lieser decided to dine out and entered the Zähringer Hof. After he had dined he remained at the table and drank beer while he read the newspaper. While he was sitting there another man came and sat at the same table. His name was Ludwig Parkratz Zind and he was a teacher at the Grimmelshausen Gymnasium, and quite a local celebrity. They entered into conversation which soon degenerated, on Zind's part, into a typically Nazi denunciation of the Jews and ended in a brawl. This incident was later to cause quite a sensation throughout the civilized world but not until a year after it took place. The most sinister aspect of the whole affair was that although Offenburg was quite a small place and Zind was well-known and the brawl which took place was the talk of the town, no mention of it appeared in the local newspaper. Had it not come to the notice of a correspondent of *Der Spiegel* nothing would have ever been heard about it.

In December 1957 an article appeared in *Der Spiegel* under the headline "Israel should be eradicated" setting out much of the conversation between Zind and Lieser. According to the writer of the article, and practically none of the conversation was ever disputed at the trial which took place four months later, it might have come straight from Julius Streicher's anti-Semitic rag, *Der Sturmer*. It consisted of the old nonsense about the Nordic race and the *untermenschen* (sub-humans), and also the approval by Zind not only of the Nuremberg racial laws but of the steps taken by Himmler to implement them by exterminating the Jews. According to the report in *Der Spiegel* the confrontation between this unfortunate Jew and his rabid Nazi table companion ended explosively in the following exchanges.

Lieser. You as a teacher should feel ashamed of your statement. I suspect that you would even have the audacity to praise the Nazi mass murder.

Zind. In my opinion far too few Jews went into the gas chambers.

Lieser. This is outrageous! Do you know that I spent the war in a concentration camp, that I was tortured and beaten and that I almost lost my voice.

Zind. What? That means they forgot to gas you too? It is a pity that you did not go up in smoke like the others.

Lieser. Today you would put me in a concentration camp if you had your way, wouldn't you?

Zind. Why not? And let me add this; I would not hesitate to kill you!

Lieser. And what about my wife? Would you gas her too?

Zind. Of course I would! It could all be done at the same time.

Lieser. What would you do with my two children?

Zind. For my part they could stay alive, but let me tell you this: I am proud that during the war I and my men killed hundreds of Jews with shovel blows on the skull. I would not hesitate to do it again.

Lieser then jumped at Zind's throat and called him a murderer to which Zind replied, "You dirty Jew".

When all this evidence was given at the trial the only part of the conversation which was disputed by the accused was the statement about killing Jews. He explained to the Court that they were Russians whom he and his men had murdered in this way.

The trial which took place in Offenberg itself caused repercussions everywhere. It was not true that there was anything special about Zind. There were many like him in Germany then, and there are still many today. What was unfortunate was the effect which this outbreak of anti-Semitism might have on world opinion for at that time every effort was being made to assure Germany's former enemies that everything had changed, that Nazism was dead and buried, and that none of these things could ever happen again. It was very unpopular in England, at any rate in political circles, even to suggest that perhaps it was a little too early to be sure of this, and that people like Dr. Conant, the first U.S. Ambassador to the Federal German Republic were a little over-optimistic when they said, as he did, that "taking all the facts into consideration it seems to be quite clear that the myth of the Third Reich has been destroyed, and that Free Germany today repudiates the Nazi past".

It was for this reason that every effort had been made to hush up the Zind incident by the Ministry of Higher Education in Baden-Wurtemberg and by the Minister of Justice. Even before it got as far as that attempts had been made to stifle it at the lowest level. The school authorities had tried to get the matter settled by persuading Zind to apologize to Lieser, but he refused. "I would rather clean the streets", he told them, "than crawl to a Jew."*

Like so many other Nazis Zind soon found a new home after he had been convicted and sentenced to a year's imprisonment. He escaped to Egypt where, doubtless, he received an enthusiastic welcome from another confirmed Jew hater, President Nasser.

During his trial Zind had shown no regret whatsoever for his behaviour. He still adhered to the political concepts of National Socialism and like many other Germans, including Adolf von Thadden, he only blamed Hitler for losing the war.

It was not only the foreign press, which reacted strongly to the Zind case. Some of the leading German newspapers were also very critical and not a little perturbed. The *Frankfurter Rundschau* stated that there were thousands of Zinds who "gave unabashed vent to their feelings in the Bierstuben. The anti-Semitic exchanges that one hears are quite revolting. They always end with statements like: 'Not enough Jews were gassed', or, 'They should be exterminated like vermin'."

In vino veritas: unfortunately there is no Latin word for beer.

The *Suddeutsche Zeitung* was even more outspoken and stated what many knew but did not dare to say in public:

> The circumstances of the Zind Case [the article stated] have brought to light that the conditions in Germany are worse than most of us dare to say. The alarming fact is that the German people today are deeply confused in their concepts of right and wrong . . . There is widespread praise of Zind as an "upright character" who dared to stick to his opinion and would "rather clean the streets than crawl before a Jew". We wonder whether this is the voice of an oversensitive national conscience or only the conspiracy of our society standing on the principle that "one crow does not scratch the eyes of another".

It had not taken very long after the end of the Allied occupation of Western Germany for the old Nazis to come out into the open. During the next two years there were to be further

*See report of the trial in the *Frankfurter Allgemeine Zeitung*, April 10-12, 1958.

disturbing outbreaks of anti-Semitism which embarrassed the Bonn government greatly and especially Chancellor Adenauer who had done so much to persuade the Americans, the British and the French that there was no possible chance of a Nazi revival and that in Germany the other N.A.T.O. powers would find a reliable and faithful ally.

The Zind case was not the only one of its kind as the *Frankfurter Rundschau* and the *Suddeutsche Zeitung* emphasized. There was one other which also attracted a great deal of publicity and was reported at length in the magazine *Look* in May 1959. This concerned a Jewish family named Sumpf in the small town of Köppern in Hesse. They had been living in Israel and returned to Germany in 1957 so that their old father could realize his greatest wish which was to see the Vaterland once more before he died. They opened a cafe in Köppern and one evening a group of rowdy former Nazis came in and began to insult the Sumpfs. The following is an extract from the article in the magazine.

> One of the gang, Reinhold Katzorke, the son of a well known former stormtrooper had brought five friends with him to the cafe. They had been drinking. Suddenly Katzorke started shouting at Frau Sumpf and began molesting the waitresses. When her husband tried to restrain him the others joined in the scuffle. "Let's shoot the Jew", someone cried. "He isn't worth a bullet", another jeered. Somehow, with the aid of other patrons, Herr Sumpf forced the men into the street. When he looked out a few minutes later to see if they had gone away a shot rang out and a bullet whistled by his head. The local police did not think that the incident was worth investigating . . . Today the Stumpf family is ruined, their nerves are shattered, their savings gone and their hopes crushed. Herr Sumpf has been shot at, his wife beaten and his son bullied. Their business is boycotted by Köppern's inhabitants.
>
> All this is for one reason only: the Sumpfs are Jews.

Although the German authorities tried to maintain that the story in *Look* was grossly exaggerated charges had subsequently to be brought against eleven defendants among them members of the local police.

It is said by some people that it is wrong to draw any premature conclusions from incidents like these, however many of them there may be, regarding the stability of democracy in Germany and the possibility of a resurgence of Nazism. It is surely just as wrong, and infinitely more dangerous, to dismiss them as mere hooliganism, for it may well be asked, why is it that German hooligans invariably choose Jews for their victims. A much sounder view has been expressed by Professor Richard Hiscocks of the University of Manitoba in his book *Democracy in Western Germany*, which was written in 1957.

> It takes time to build a democratic tradition and there has not been sufficient time since 1945 . . . The struggle for democracy, therefore, is largely in the future, with tradition, apathy and self-satisfaction as the main obstacles to be overcome. Those who paint too favourable a picture and over-emphasize what has been achieved may do as much or more harm than others who from time to time have exaggerated Communist or neo-Nazi dangers.
>
> Underrating the difficulties of democracy is no service to the democratic cause. Rather it encourages the self-deception of anti-democrats who are only too ready to accept a low estimate of a system they dislike, and discourages true democrats who are aware of present imperfections and of the path that has yet to be travelled.

"The path that has yet to be travelled". Anyone who has tried to study the history of Western Germany since 1945 with any objectivity cannot be unaware that true German democrats have still a long way to go before they reach the end of the road.

CHAPTER THREE

The Return of the Swastika

UNTIL THE last few days of 1959 anyone who foresaw or predicted a revival of Nazism in the Federal Republic was regarded as an unreasonable pessimist or even, in some cases, as an unrepentant German-hater. So long as Germany remained prosperous, they said, there was very little danger that the new democracy in Western Germany would share the fate of the Weimar Republic and, "should the boom go on until a new generation has grown up, democracy would be safe".* There was some foundation for such criticism although anyone with a knowledge of German history might well have been forgiven for having some apprehension for the future.

However the anti-Semitic and Nazi outbreaks which began on the night of Christmas Eve 1959 and continued until January 28th 1960 provided some grounds for this "premature" pessimism.

About 11 p.m., on the memorial stone erected in Cologne in the Hansaring for the victims of National-Socialism bearing the inscription

Here lie seven victims of the Gestapo
This memorial recalls Germany's most shameful period
1933-1945

the second sentence was smeared over with black varnish paint.

During the same night, on Christmas Day, towards 2.30 a.m. the synagogue in the Roonstrasse in Cologne was besmirched by the following inscriptions.

(1) The outside wall of the synagogue by the words "Out with the Jews", and, "Germans say: Out with the Jews".

*See "The reappearance of the Swastika", a pamphlet by J. Jaeger, published by Gamma Publications Ltd.

(*above*) Adolf von Thadden, Chairman of N.P.D., signs autographs in Nuremberg. (*right*) Otto Remer, post-war leader of the S.R.P.

(*left*) Dr Hans Globke with Dr Adenauer at the Chancellory. (*below left*) Dr Werner Naumann, arrested for plotting in 1953. (*below right*) The present German Chancellor, Herr Kiesinger

(2) A wall and one entrance to the synagogue by Swastikas and by daubing over the words "Cologne Synagogue Community".

(3) The inside of the porch by a swastika and also by painting over the bell-plate and the door handle.

For this smearing, red and white varnish paint was used. On the strength of an anonymous telephone call and certain information given by the acting President of the Cologne District Association of the D.R.P. (the Deutsche Reichs Partei) the police arrested within a few hours a suspect, Arnold Strunk, aged 23. After a brief interrogation he admitted having been responsible for both these acts. Three hours later another young man, named Paul Schonen, aged 25, was also arrested. At first he denied any participation in these incidents but on December 28th he admitted being an accessory to the offence. Both these men lived together in the house of Schonen's father who was a wholesale paper merchant whose customers included the Cologne Synagogue Community.

Schonen did not think that a democracy was the most suitable form of government for Germans and preferred what he called a "moderate dictatorship", and for this reason he had joined the D.R.P. after attending one of its meetings and, a few months later, his friend Strunk also became a member. Strunk had for a long time been interested in anti-Semitic books and pamphlets and although he did not go along with Hitler to the extent of thinking that the Jews should be exterminated he was in favour of expelling them from the Federal Republic.

These two young men adorned their rooms with Nazi emblems, D.R.P. posters, and pictures of Hitler and Horst Wessel. They also had a cupboard which was painted black, white and red. The room also contained a large collection of pro-Nazi books including the following: *Mein Kampf; Hitler the General; Pictures of the Waffen S.S.; Leadership and Obedience*, and a D.R.P. publication entitled *Judges and anti-Semites*. The room was known amongst other members of the D.R.P. as "The Brown House", and it became a meeting place for many of its members also, where they listened to the records of Nazi speeches and songs and held political discussions.

Prior to the Christmas incidents both these men had committed other similar offences. On a lavatory door in a Cologne bank slogans had been painted, and on another the words

"Down with Adenauer and his arse-kissing policy" had also been daubed.

Had these been the only outbreaks of anti-Semitism the Federal Government might have been able to ignore them and the outside world would not have taken much notice. But it became infectious and by January 28th there had been 470 further incidents not including 215 cases of mere scribblings by children who had decided to join in the "fun". By no means all the culprits were discovered; 234 were arrested of whom no less than 144 were between the ages of 16 and 30. This meant that none of them had been more than sixteen years of age when the war ended, a fact which shook the confidence of those optimists who had been saying that if the boom in Germany continued until such time as a new generation had grown up democracy would be safe. Moreover all the offenders with the exception of three were German nationals. Out of the total number of cases where those who had committed these offences were identified 138 were the work of people whose attitude to the present constitution was hostile and nearly all of them were directed against the Jews. Posters carrying anti-Jewish slogans such as "Down with the Jews! To the gas chambers!" were thrown into taverns, houses and shops owned or occupied by Jews, and swastikas were painted on many buildings including Synagogues, Churches and Jewish cemeteries. Anonymous letters were sent to many employers demanding that all Jews in their employ should be dismissed, and to many Jewish families, and threatening nocturnal telephone calls were also received by many Jews. 239 cases involved the smearing of Nazi and anti-Jewish slogans on dwelling houses, factory buildings, barracks, cinemas, telephone booths, bridges, traffic signs, railway carriages, motor cars and even trees. The most common of these slogans were "Out with the Jews" and "*Heil* Hitler". Of the total number of offences committed between Christmas Day and January 28th 1960 70 per cent were either Nazi or anti-Semitic.

These outbreaks of anti-Semitism were of such magnitude that they could not be ignored by the Federal Government and statements were made, while they were still going on, by the Chancellor Dr. Adenauer over the German radio and television networks and by the Vice-President of the Bundestag, Dr. Carlo Schmidt four days later.

The Chancellor said that the desecration of the synagogue and the memorial to victims of Nazi persecution had "produced here in Germany a wave of indignation against those responsible and in some other countries a wave of hatred against all Germans and particularly against the Germany of today". He told those who were listening to him both at home and abroad that he was especially qualified to say this because he and his family had themselves been victims of National-Socialism and that his name had figured four times on a list of persons condemned to death by the Nazis. Moreover, when he and his family were in great financial straits during the Nazi régime it was two Jews who were the first to offer him financial assistance. When he became Chancellor one of the first things he did was to promote the Restitution Agreement with Israel* and in doing so he wished to show the whole world that present day Germany absolutely rejected anti-Semitism.

When the Chancellor said this he was, of course, speaking sincerely and frankly. There were many other Germans, however, who were only indignant against those responsible because of the unpleasant publicity which these incidents had created abroad. Unfortunately, however, the Chancellor then went on to say that nearly all the incidents had been committed by hooligans and that they "appeared to have no political background", and the White Paper which was subsequently published by the Federal Government devoted a number of pages, as will be seen later in this chapter, in trying to shift the blame on to the Communists who had been for years carrying on a propaganda campaign designed to slander the Federal Republic before the eyes of the world presenting it as fascist, militarist and revanchist.

The statement made by Dr. Carlo Schmidt, who is a member of the S.D.P., was much more forthright and he did not attempt to put the blame on other shoulders. For this reason it is set out in full below as it represents the views of one of those, and although they are not over popular there are, fortunately more than a few of them, who are determined to do all in their power to ensure that democracy in Germany shall succeed and that

*The Basic Principles of the N.P.D. deplore the pouring out "in distant lands of thousands of millions which serve neither German nor European interests" and "the continued payment of camouflaged reparation".

there must never be a return to the shameful days of the Third Reich.

This is what Dr. Schmidt said:

On the night before Christmas, abominable characters besmeared the place of worship of the Jewish community in Cologne with swastikas and anti-Semitic abuse. Since then there have been further cases of similar daubings of an anti-Semitic or Nazi nature. The Government will certainly submit all pertinent material to the Bundestag.

That this could happen in our country is a disgrace—a disgrace which is in no way diminished by the fact that in other countries, too, walls have been besmirched with swastikas and vilifications of the Jewish people. We Germans have no right to point at others: elsewhere there have certainly been gross acts committed under the swastika; in our country, however, six million Jews were murdered under that sign. For this reason what has happened in the past weeks is more shameful here than elsewhere. For this reason our reaction against it, both moral and with the lictor's fasces, must be stronger, and springs from deeper perceptions than with others. Of course it is certain that the excesses of which we are ashamed had many different causes and instigators. In some cases herostratic megalomania, the desire to appear on the news-reel and in the papers may have played a part. In some cases political sectarianism was at work which may in addition have been planned from somewhere behind the scenes. In other cases juvenile hooliganism was evident. Yet, these facts should not set our minds at rest. The fact that these juveniles, most of whom were less than ten years old in 1945 and have never seen a Jew face to face, instead of releasing their surplus energy by overturning cars and breaking windows did so by scrawling anti-Semitic slogans reveals that there is still some garbage lying around in the sub-conscience of many. This may be the fault of parents; it may be the fault of teachers; inferiority complexes may be responsible; perhaps a moral environment may still be found here and there, which conjures up such phantoms.

That this is so concerns all of us. This is a task for us all and if we fail, then our people will never recover. As long as someone in Germany can state, without having to fear that people will turn their backs on him, that the way the Third Reich behaved towards the Jews was very stupid because it turned the whole world against us; as long as people here can discuss, with an exculpatory intention, whether six million or "only" three million Jews were murdered; as long as every child has not been taught and made to understand that the problem is not whether six or three million, but whether none or one was murdered; as long as all this can happen, we—even those of us who kept their hands clean during that infamous time—have failed. And above all we shall have failed as long as we do not consider what was done to the synagogues in the first place from the moral standpoint, but consider it from the aspect of the harm it may have done to the Federal Republic.

Many have regretted that the press gave so much publicity to this dirty business—particularly many members of Jewish communities have done so. All the fuss certainly incited a dozen more teddy-boys—but perhaps this was a good thing. For there are situations in which one must waken the sleeping hell-hounds in order to realize fully from their howlings how close we still are to the inferno.

Only by dissipating the dark forces which still exert their evil influence here and there among our people shall we be able to banish them. Certainly other people should also help us: they should not only see the offences, but also the reactions of countless people, and especially the countless young people amongst us. These must be encouraged; we must not make these young people feel that they stand alone or that they are even counted among the outlaws. We should stand by them fraternally. If we do this, then the phantoms will also vanish from our midst.

Freedom and truth are at stake in the matters of which I am speaking—not merely in an academic sense. We must give a living proof of these virtues in ourselves, rather as Schiller wrote to his friend Korner: "The first law is: Respect the freedom of others. The second law is: Show freedom yourself". However, there is no freedom outside the truth in which we move at all times, with everything which history has laid upon our shoulders.

If the younger generation which is growing up in Germany today will only follow Dr. Schmidt's advice the chance that the other Germany will one day rise again is extremely remote.

This outbreak of anti-Semitic feeling in Germany, and in a number of other countries, however insignificant it may have appeared to some people caused considerable apprehension even in Germany and disturbed the confidence which many people were beginning to have in the new but as yet untried democratic régime in the Federal German Republic.

That it began in Germany and was immediately taken up in

many other countries, including, in a minor degree, the United Kingdom should not have occasioned any surprise. There is nothing new about anti-Semitism and it has been practised before by the extreme Left as well as the extreme Right. One should never forget the "Protocols of the Elders of Zion"* and there are anti-Semitic Groups and organizations in many other countries beside Germany. They are not, however, of any great significance, but German anti-Semitism, as many West German newspapers freely admitted at the time, is different.

When there had been a similar, though not so serious an outbreak just over a year earlier *Die Welt* discussed the special significance of the outrages and dealt with the assertion, which had been made by many Germans that it was all the work of the Communists. The Germans, the paper stated, had enforced special racial hatred with an obstinate and obsessed determination and in so doing had "demonstrated its absurdity". That was why, the article continued, any anti-Semitic utterance by a German had a ring different from any similar utterance by a Briton, a Frenchman or a Swede. The Germans had "lost all innocence and could never claim to be free from bias so far as the Jews were concerned".

On the earlier occasion Dr. Adenauer, during a debate in the Bundestag, "profoundly deplored" the incidents, but no action was taken. When the symptoms reappeared on Christmas Eve 1959 many Germans as well as those outside Western Germany began to ask themselves these questions. Is there a resurgence of the Nazi ideology in the Federal Republic today. If so, how serious is it, what are its causes and what should be done by the Germans themselves to put an end to it?

In a leading article in *The Times* it was stated that such tendencies could only be eliminated through the education of the German people and, in particular, by the removal, from positions where they can influence the young, of those who still hold Nazi beliefs.

It cannot be denied that there are men in the present administration in Western Germany whose past political record

*A document, palpably a forgery, which suddenly came into existence towards the end of World War I and the origin of which is still obscure. It purported to reveal a Jewish conspiracy to rule the world. It was resurrected during the Third Reich by Julius Streicher, "Jew-baiter Number One", as he liked to be called, and it was used in anti-Semitic propaganda and taught in schools.

is none too savoury and who, many Germans feel should not be there.* There are even more of them in positions of less responsibility, in the judiciary, in the Civil Service, in industry and, above all, in the teaching profession.† Even though there is at present no likelihood of Jews being persecuted in Germany, even if only for the reason that there are so few of them, there is an urgent need for the Germans to realize that the danger of the revival of Nazism is still possible in certain circumstances. This realization will never come about while there is the prevalent tendency not merely to forget the terrible past, but even to pretend that it never existed. If the ever increasing evidence of a growing desire to slur over the past is doing "regrettable harm to Germany's reputation abroad", to use Dr. Adenauer's own words, the Germans have only themselves to blame for the facts speak for themselves.

A television feature in Western Germany which was shown during the summer of 1959, entitled "Eyes on our Youth", revealed that nine out of ten schoolboys knew nothing about Hitler except that he made the autobahns, cured unemployment and organized the "Strength through Joy" cruises. Only one in ten knew that millions of Jews were murdered and a group of young teachers and undergraduates, when asked about what the world now knows as Hitler's "Final Solution of the Jewish Question" put the number killed at a paltry forty thousand.

Such ignorance was hardly surprising when many of the history text books used in West German schools either omitted altogether or glossed over the Nazis' barbarous crimes. Shortly after these outbreaks of anti-Semitism an inquiry was ordered by the Minister of Education in Hesse into the instruction given to children in the secondary schools about the period 1933-45. An examination of the text books used in the senior forms revealed that as a general rule the history masters never managed to reach this "delicate chapter" as the *Frankfurter Neue Press* called it.

Furthermore, under the caption of "Humiliating Figures", *Die Welt* published the following statistics revealing the space allotted to the recent past in two different editions of a widely

*There still are such men in the present administration.

†See pages 92–113.

used German history text book, one published in 1949 and the other in 1958.

Subject	1949 *pages*	1958 *pages*
History of the Hitler regime	41	13
The Reichstag Fire	$2\frac{1}{2}$	NIL
Persecution of the Jews	3	14 lines
Resistance movement	8	NIL
Concentration camps	5	NIL
Nazi persecution of religion	2	$4\frac{1}{2}$ lines

These figures speak for themselves. Nevertheless the difficulties which face many teachers are not unreal, for if they attempt to enlighten their pupils, as some of them do, they often receive strong support from the press but none from the children's parents who appear to resent, perhaps in some cases to fear the truthful presentation of the facts.

Immediately after the events which have been described earlier in this chapter there was universal condemnation of them by the President, the Chancellor, the Churches and many responsible people in public life, and a few months later a White Paper was issued by the German Government entitled "The Anti-Semitic and Nazi incidents from December 25th 1959 until January 28th 1960". Although these incidents were fully dealt with in the White Paper and were, quite properly condemned, several pages were devoted to an attempt to put much blame on "Right-wing radicals and Communist elements", and referred to the attempt to discredit the Federal Republic in the eyes of the world made by the Communists for many years. The object of such propaganda, it was stated in the White Paper, was to represent the Federal Republic to its Western partners and Eastern neighbours as a disturber of peace to isolate it already during the preparations for the Summit conference and thus to open the way for recognition of the Soviet occupied zone.*

The remainder of this section of the White Paper (Section E, Evaluation of the Incidents) was devoted to playing down what it described as "The home aspect". Among the offenders, it was stated, there were "convinced anti-Semites", who "made no

*This is the Federal German Republic's name for D.D.R. (Deutsches Democratische Republik) or what is usually known in Britain as East Germany.

bones about their anti-Jewish views and did not hesitate to abuse their Jewish fellow citizens". The development of their political views was attributed to their having been "influenced by anti-Semitic and Right-Wing literature". The White Paper finally assured the German public, if many of them bothered to read it, that the proportion of offenders who had acted from political motives was only 8 per cent. Two thirds of the incidents was "simply a question of rowdy hooliganism". Furthermore thirteen of the offences had been committed "in a state of complete pathological delirium or by reason of other psycopathological disorders". One of these was a man who made anti-Semitic speeches in the Hamburg University library and afterwards, as he left the building greeted a number of people with the Hitler salute. One's memory does not have to go back very far to recall the Führer's anti-Semitic speeches all over the country and the wild cheering with which they were greeted by millions of his admirers. Others who sang Nazi songs and greeted police officers with the Nazi salute were described as having done so in order to "bolster their self-esteem in their relations with the authorities". Furthermore, even those who had committed these offences because of their avowed anti-Semitic view had done so because they were in "an advanced state of intoxication". But perhaps the most significant of these excuses was that "for want of other forms of expression Nazi symbols and slogans were used to protest against the democratic form of government without any discernible simultaneous intent of glorifying National Socialism".

It is not to be wondered at that some Germans had then, and still have, fears about the future of their country. They remember that when Goethe was once asked "what is Germany?", he replied, "I do not know, for there are two Germanys, and where spiritual Germany ends political Germany begins" and they had genuine fears that the spiritual Germany of which Goethe spoke would not prevail and that with rearmament of Germany there could eventually come a resurgence of the old military spirit and an opportunity would arise for many still unrepentant Nazis to obtain control. It is to be hoped that these Germans are wrong and that the spiritual Germany of which Goethe spoke will get her chance, for it may be the last.

Everyone should know what the "other" Germany wants. In

1955 Field-Marshal Kesselring was released from prison where he had been serving a life sentence as a war criminal for his part in the massacre of over three hundred Italian civilians in the Ardeatine Caves. At the time of his release the British Government announced that it was due to ill health and that he was suffering from "cardiac trouble". Nevertheless, it did not prevent him, when he was President of the Stahlhelm, from travelling all over Germany making provocative militaristic speeches at ex-servicemen's rallies. At one of these, and it is typical of them all, one of the delegates who was a member of the Ruhr Parliament said, "We want to bring back to Germany the old spirit of the Prussians. All this talk of a democratic army is nonsense. It must be the Prussian system again. This was the system which created tough men at arms. If the world wants our soldiers let us train them in our own way. The army must, once more become the first Estate of the Realm."

If that were to come about it would mean the end of the present regime in Germany. The Weimar Republic would not have lasted as long as it did, and that was less than fifteen years had it not co-operated with the German General Staff and permitted German militarism to restore German military strength. Similarly the Federal German Republic would not last long should, as the "other" Germany wants, the Army once more become the master of the State and not its servant.

Even at the present time there is no real reason to suppose that it is in any way imminent, but there is cause for some uneasiness for there is reason to believe, as will be seen later, that the N.P.D.,* and particularly its basic principles as set out in the Party's Manifesto, is popular with a very large number of officers in the Bundeswehr and that as time goes on, unless there is a radical change of thinking in Germany, this Party will receive considerable support from the Bundeswehr between now and the general election in September 1968. The main reason for suspecting that this may happen is the fact that three of the most important planks in N.P.D. policy are the denial of war guilt, the assertion that the courageous conduct of German soldiers throughout the ages must be the model for the Bundeswehr, and the emphasis that Germany is entitled to the territories in which the German *volk* has had its roots for

*The National Democratic Party in the Federal German Republic.

centuries. In the words of the Manifesto, "there cannot be a united pacified Europe without a reunited independent Germany. Therefore first Germany, then Europe!
GERMANY FOR THE GERMANS—EUROPE FOR THE EUROPEANS.

Furthermore there are some ominous and significant indications that the old system might eventually gain control. The Waffen S.S., who did most of the dirty work for the Wehrmacht are now eligible for service in the Bundeswehr, nor is this all. For some time there has been a tendency to whitewash them and to forget the abominable crimes for which they were directly responsible in Europe. The Nuremberg Tribunal in its judgment declared the Waffen S.S. a "criminal organization" upon the best evidence, but General Manteuffel when he was a member of the Bundestag spoke of them publicly as "magnificent fellows" and Herr Strauss, the present Finance Minister in the Coalition Government and Kiesinger's right hand man said, "You surely know what I think of the conduct of the units of the Waffen S.S. who served at the front. Of course I extend to them the high honour I accord to German soldiers of the last World War."

It is this attitude of mind on the part of several Germans some of whom are members of the present government in the F.D.R. which brings despair into the hearts of those in Germany, and there are more than a few of them, who do not want to go back to the bad old days.

Another discomforting feature is that even today, when no one need be ignorant of the facts, provided they want to know them, there is very little shame in Germany, except amongst the young, the majority of whom say that they cannot understand how their parents and grandparents "fell for Hitler".* This is not the same as saying that the Germans bear a collective guilt for those crimes. It would be ridiculous to expect those who were yet unborn or who were still young when all these atrocities were committed to bear any guilt. Nevertheless, there should be a general acknowledgment that these crimes took place, a regret that they were committed, and a determination on the part of all Germans not to let the opportunity arise for their repetition. The cause and effect of the tendency on the part of those who are responsible for educating the German youth of today to minimize the past has already been dealt with above.

*See pages 161–2, 169.

CHAPTER FOUR

Voices from the Past

Before 1950, denazification, which has been well described as the grand illusion of the immediate post-war period, had practically ended, and for all the good it had accomplished it might as well never have been carried out, for it proved to be entirely ineffective. All the lesser Nazis and nearly all the important ones had not only been released from the internment camps, but were free to carry on as they had left off in 1945. It is difficult to understand how the Allied powers could have imagined that denazification could possibly have any lasting effect unless they intended to occupy Germany for at least one generation. What happened, of course, was that from 1951 onwards former Nazis began to be reinstated in public life and this has continued ever since. It is true that many Germans had been members of the party in name only, because they had to join it in order to keep their jobs, and that their reinstatement was unlikely to constitute any danger. But it was not only they who came back into government service. The real dedicated Nazis began to play an important role in West Germany, in government, in industry, in banking, in the press and education, and it is they who are the voices from the past. It was, of course, argued, as it was bound to be, that men with experience of business and administration were essential if the new democratic State was to be run efficiently. Nevertheless, it is unfortunate that so many of those who held diplomatic posts under von Ribbentrop have been similarly employed during the last sixteen years, and this was excused by the former Chancellor, Dr. Adenauer, on the grounds that a new foreign office could not be built with amateurs. Professionals were essential even if they had served under von Ribbentrop. In Adenauer's government at least two former Nazis held the rank of Minister. The Minister of the Interior, Herr Jerhard Schroder, had been a member of the Storm Troopers (S.A.) and Herr Theodor Oberlander, who was Minister of Refugees, was formerly an S.S. Captain in the Wlassow Army.

The appointment which has met with the most criticism, however, and with good reason, was that of Hans Globke. It was during the trial of Adolf Eichmann* that the news that he had written the official Nazi commentary on the Nuremberg Race Laws in 1935 became known to the public. "For the first time", according to the *Neue Zurchen Zeitung* of May 15th 1961, "the name Globke was mentioned in connection with the persecution of the Jews during the war", but an explanation was immediately issued by what is always termed "a spokesman" of the German Chancellor's office to the effect that Doctor Globke had attended the conference which had been referred to by one of the witnesses at Eichmann's trial "only in the capacity of an observer at the request of resistance movement circles".

In an extremely well documented book, written by a Polish writer Jan Zaborowski, he discusses the question of whether Globke was merely a passive "observer" or was he the co-author of the legislation which led to the extermination of the Jews. Did he act "at the request of resistance movement circles", or was he an active collaborator and formulator of laws of the Third Reich?†

There would appear to be ample evidence that Dr. Globke's role in formulating the policy of national segregation in the Third Reich was by no means a minor one, as will be seen later, and it was, therefore, surprising that when called as a witness at one of the Nuremberg Trials, which is generally known as "The Ministries Trial" he tried to maintain that the Nuremberg Laws were not the legal basis for the prosecution of the Jews which, in the words of Cassandra, of the *Daily Mirror*, "led to the gas ovens of Auschwitz and all the unspeakable abominations of the concentration camps". It is abundantly clear that they were, and were intended to be, and Globke admitted in a television interview in 1961 that he "co-operated temporarily in working out the initial enforcing regulations to the 'Reich Citizenship Law'

*See the *Trial of Adolf Eichmann* (Heinemann) by the author, who attended the trial in Jerusalem.
†Doctor Hans Globke, *The Good Clerk*, by Jan Zaborowski (1961).

and 'The Law for the Protection of German blood and German honour'." That his "temporary co-operation" was whole-hearted is proved by a letter which was written by Wilhelm Frick to Rudolf Hess on April 25th 1935. "Senior Ministerial Counsellor, Dr. Globke", Frick wrote "is undoubtedly one of the most capable and hard working officials in my Ministry. He played an outstanding part in the creation of the following laws", mentioning the laws referred to above. In reward for Globke's co-operation Frick asked Hess to promote him because "he played a quite outstanding part in the creation of these laws". Although Globke has frequently stated that he tried to modify some of the suggestions made by Rudolf Hess and others for inclusion in the Nuremberg Laws, such as the question of mixed blood (i.e. Jews who were the offspring of mixed marriages) and that there is some evidence to support this assertion, there can be no doubt that he was not just an *innocent* collaborator. He was asked by the prosecutor in the "Ministries Trial" whether it was true that whereas Wilhelm Stuckart wrote the preface it was he himself who had written the commentary, to which he replied, "That is correct". To appreciate what this meant it is necessary to recall briefly some of the points contained in the commentary.

The first concerned the question of protecting domestic servants from the "racially pernicious sexual threats of their Jewish employers or Jewish lodgers". The second dealt with the Aryan partner of a mixed marriage who decided to adopt, *even temporarily*, the Jewish faith, in respect of which Globke laid down that any child of such a marriage would be treated as a "full Jew" and there could be no appeal against this decision. The third forbade Catholics of Jewish birth to be married in church. This was introduced by Globke on his own initiative but since he wrote the commentary he appears to have changed his mind, for some years after the war ended he said that he was now of the opinion that it was "repugnant and loathsome".*

With the outbreak of war on September 1st 1939 Counsellor Globke's duties changed and are set out in a document which is in existence today issued by the Ministry of the Interior on January 29th 1940 which stated, "Dr. Hans Globke, Ministerial Counsellor in the Reich Ministry of the Interior . . . cannot be

*As reported in *Der Spiegel* in April 1956.

spared. He is employed in the office of the General Plenipotentiary for Reich Administration and is an expert on matters of citizenship arising from the establishment of the Protectorate, incorporation of the territories of the East, formation of the general Government and resettlement campaigns". This bureaucratic verbiage meant in plain language that he was actively engaged, sitting behind a desk, in preparing the final stage, after the defeat of the Poles, of the segregation of the population in Poland, and everyone knows that the word "resettlement" used in this context was one of the charming euphemisms used by the Nazis for sending the Jews to the gas chambers of camps like Auschwitz, Treblinka, Chelmo and Sobidor.

The defence put forward by all these Nazi civil servants is exactly the same as that made at all the war crime trials by war criminals who served during the war in one of the services, namely the defence of superior orders. They say that they were just "good clerks". They did not formulate these policies, nor did they carry them out. All they did was to communicate them from their authors to the Generals, the Gauleiters, the S.S. and the Gestapo, and no blame can be attached to them.

The defence of superior orders has no legal basis whatsoever. In 1919 an International Commission was appointed to consider and report to the Allied powers on the question of immunity of heads of State in respect of the conduct of the war. The report stated that the civil and military authorities cannot be relieved from responsibility by the mere fact that a higher authority might have been convicted of the same offence. Even the German Code of Military Law provided that a soldier must execute all orders undeterred by the fear of legal consequences, but it added that this would not excuse him in cases where he must have known with certainty that the order was illegal. This view was held and expressed by the German Supreme Court in Leipsig in 1921. The court was trying two naval officers who had been members of the ship's company of a German U-boat which, during the 1914-18 war, had sunk the *Llandovery Castle*, a British hospital ship: In obedience to an order given by the commander of the submarine to leave no trace these two junior officers gave orders to fire on the hospital ship lifeboats. The Court, applying the German Military Code mentioned above, said in its judgment that the commander's order to leave no trace did not free the accused from guilt . . . In this case it must have been perfectly clear to the accused that killing defenceless people in the lifeboats could be nothing else but a breach of the law, and the two officers should have refused to obey the order.

The same principle must surely apply to a senior civil servant who is told to issue instructions or regulations which clearly constitute an offence against the Laws and Customs of War. It is his clear duty to say "No". In the case of a junior subordinate the decision may not be easy and this should, therefore, be taken into account as a mitigating factor.

There is no doubt that had Dr. Globke regarded what he was doing as wrong, he could have resigned and asked for a transfer to some other department. As he was only 42 years of age in 1940 he could even have left his desk and joined one of the services. There were other Germans who did this, and as he did not do so he cannot really complain of the criticism which has been levelled against him. For Dr. Adenauer to have appointed him to such an important and influential post was inexcusable and the Chancellor's persistant refusal to dismiss him was quite indefensible.

In an interview with Cassandra published in the *Daily Mirror* in June 1961, Globke said, "I was never a member of the Party. People like myself, of course, had difficulties because of this. There was heavy pressure. It came in different ways. Some could not withstand. Others were successful". For this reason, he continued, "I was not promoted with the speed I would otherwise have expected and I rose only to the rank of Ministerial Counsellor". He had to wait until West Germany became a democracy.

Nevertheless, even though his promotion was slow he held a position in his own department where he was able to influence the formulation and practical application of the policies of the Third Reich. Jan Zaborowski, in the book referred to above, sums up Globke's twelve years in the government service of the Third Reich in these words:

> He was not only actively engaged in the practice of Nazism, implementing its programme by way of laws and administration measures but he also:

The desecration of a Jewish cemetery in Bamberg in 1965

Dr Otto Ambros confers happily with his lawyer during his trial in Nuremberg in 1947

Alfred Krupp, the German industrialist, during his trial at Nuremberg for war crimes

> Firstly, took part in the implementation of the most inhuman and most absurd—but precisely for this reason the most tragic in their consequences—points of the Nazi programme; racialism, "nationality struggle", the creation of a privileged status for Germans in Europe and the subjugation of other nations;
>
> Secondly, thanks to his intelligence and knowledge, and his ability to perceive the true meaning of every policy through the regulations he drafted, he fulfilled not only the individual or immediate objectives of the Nazi Party and the Government of the Third Reich, but the fundamental and final goals of Nazism;
>
> And thirdly, as an outstanding official and experienced specialist on law and administration, he gave invaluable service to the régime.

There is no disputing the fact that he knew what he was doing and what was going on all around him. He knew that his masters were criminals such as had not been seen for hundreds of years, yet he had the audacity to tell Cassandra that he knew and all other Germans knew, that Jews were transported to the East, but that he did not know that they "were being put to death *en masse*". He occupied a post in the Ministry of the Interior where this information was, undoubtedly, available and he must have had access to it.

The past connections of the present Chancellor of the Federal Republic with the Third Reich are not of such a nature as to increase the hope in many German breasts that the new democracy in West Germany will survive the trials and tribulations which may well beset it during the next two decades, and there are many who were surprised at his appointment and were by no means happy about it.

Herr Kiesinger joined the Nazi Party in 1933 and was employed as a "scientific assistant" in the Foreign Office and, within a short space of time, was promoted to the appointment of deputy chief of the radio policy department in the same Ministry. This department, according to the Führer's Decree of September 8th 1939, was responsible for the implementation of the directives and instructions for the foreign propaganda of the German broadcasting system which were issued. Herr Kiesinger has repeatedly said that he was never a Nazi by conviction. Nevertheless, he jumped on the band wagon at the right time and the denazification tribunal by whom his antecedents were investigated in March 1947 confirmed this by alloting him to Group IV as a Fellow Traveller. When he took part in an interview by an Israeli journalist, which appeared in a Tel Aviv newspaper and was reprinted in *Vorwarts* in February 1967, he was asked whether it was possible to resign from the Party to which he replied that he could have done so between 1934 and 1935 but that he did not then foresee the course of history. If he ever possessed a copy of *Mein Kampf* it is clear that at that time he had not read it.

In addition to his other duties as deputy chief of the radio policy department he was responsible for liaison between his office and the Propaganda Ministry of which Goebbels was the head, which conducted a continuous campaign of racial hatred and false information all over the world. No one can, of course, predict what kind of a German Chancellor Herr Kiesinger will turn out to be but there are two factors which do not encourage over-optimism. When the celebrated German novelist Gunter Grass urged him not to accept the office of Chancellor lest it should damage the Federal Republic's reputation abroad he stated that he had decided to do so provided he could get a member of the German resistance (Willy Brandt) into his Cabinet, and when asked at a press conference in Stuttgart whether he supported the demand by some Germans that the N.P.D. should be banned he replied that he did not think much of "applying executive measures in combating new emerging parties which are said to possess nationalistic tendencies". The best thing that could happen in Germany for the sake of the future would be the break-up of the present coalition between the C.D.U./C.S.U. and the Social Democrats, for Kiesinger and Brandt certainly do not come out of the same stable.

Hans Trossman, who in 1949 became Director of the West German Bundestag, is another of these voices from the past, and was from 1940 to 1942 employed in the ghetto administration at Lodz in Poland. This department was responsible for dealing with confiscated Jewish property, and during these years conditions in the ghetto were appalling. In one week alone, in February 1942, 307 Jews died from consumption, heart failure and malnutrition, and between the years 1940 and 1944 more than 43,000 died as the result of the inhuman living and working conditions.

Herr Trossman, however, had become one of the leading members of the C.S.U. by the end of 1947.

Brief summaries of the records of other former Nazis who are now in important and influential positions in Germany are given below:

(1) *Georg Vogel* who in 1961 was appointed Ambassador for the Federal Republic of Germany in Ecuador and, three years later, to the same position in Venezuela. Vogel joined the N.S.D.A.P. in 1937 and eventually reached the rank of Obersturmführer. In 1943, while holding the appointment of Counsellor in the German Legation in Athens, he was concerned in the deportation of thousands of Greek Jews. In this connection he worked in conjunction with Adolf Eichmann's department of the R.S.H.A., evidence of which was given during the Eichmann trial.* The special commando of the R.S.H.A. for the deportation of Jews from Greece to extermination camps in Poland was under the command of S.S. Hauptsturmführer Wisliceny who co-operated closely with Vogel.

By May 1943 56,000 Greek Jews had been deported of whom only 2,000 odd survived the war. In June of the same year all the property belonging to these Jews, euphemistically described as having been "left behind", was distributed on Vogel's instructions and a copy of a letter signed by him which refers to this is still in existence.

Before being appointed German Ambassador to Ecuador, Herr Vogel was a judge in West Germany from 1946 to 1949, while it was still under Allied occupation.

(2) *Dr. Walter Becher*, before 1945, when on the editorial staff of the N.S.D.A.P.'s regional journal *Die Zeit* in Czechoslovakia, was the purveyor of columns of anti-Semitic propaganda in the paper's art, science and entertainment section for which he was responsible. Its object was to make the Czechs believe that it was the Jews and not the Nazis who were the cause of their misery.

Amongst many other anti-Semitic diatribes he wrote the following: "All songs whose words originated from the Jews or which were set out to music by Jews should no longer be sung

*See Vol. 16, p. 51, of the transcript of the trial.

. . . General liberation from Judaism is the first prerequisite for the new construction of Sudeten German life. Sudetenland has become a cultural land, what was deliberately hushed up under the patronage of an unpopular government influenced by Jewish brokers can now stand up and face the general judgment."* When the war ended Becher became a foundation member of the Association of Sudeten German Fellowcountrymen, which even in those early days was pressing for the return of the Sudetenland to Germany, and in 1965, after joining the C.S.U. under Strauss he was elected to the Bundestag.

(3) *Karl Friedrich Vialon* who played quite an active part in carrying out the "Final Solution of the Jewish Question", began his bureaucratic career in the Nazi Ministry of Justice but was later transferred to the Ministry of Finance. After the fall of France in 1940 Vialon, as a senior government counsellor, helped to plunder Alsace and shortly after the invasion of Russia by Hitler in June 1941 he became head of the Finance Department of the Reich Commissariat for the Eastern Regime and set up an office in Riga. A conference was held in the Berlin suburb of Wansee in January 1942 to discuss methods of implementing the Final Solution. It was decided that "under suitable management the Jews will be brought, in the course of a final solution, to labour units in the East. Those capable of working will be transported in long labour columns, men and women separate, to build roads as a result of which a large part of them will fall out through natural losses. Those who ultimately remain must be given special treatment† (*Sonderbehandlung*) otherwise they will constitute a nucleus for the building of a new Jewry."

In consequence of this decision Himmler decreed that all Jewish people still accommodated in ghettos in the area of the Reich Commissariat for the Eastern Regions were to be transferred to concentration camps, which Vialon passed on in the following terms, "I desire that the management of the concentration camps to be erected be taken over by the general commissioner in Riga . . . the financial yields must, as previously, be paid into my treasury."

There are many documents in existence which fully support

**Die Zeit*, Reichenberg, May 23rd 1939.
†Special treatment was, of course, murder.

the above and in 1966, one hundred and twenty six were handed over by the Prosecutor General's Office in East Germany to the office in Koblenz which is responsible for conducting many of the war-crime trials in West Germany at the present time.

In 1963, when giving evidence as a witness at the trial of an S.S. mass murderer named Hausser, Vialon stated on oath that he emphatically denied having had any knowledge about any such action taken for the extermination. Vialon remained in his appointment of State Secretary until the end of 1966 and is now in receipt of a pension.

The few mentioned above in this chapter, which have been chosen at random and not because of any special significance, are only a drop in the ocean for there were many others who played equally important parts in implementing Hitler's plans to get rid of the Jews in Europe and in recent years have held important positions in the legal profession, in the diplomatic service and in industry, although the whole object of denazification was, presumably, to ensure that they should never again be employed in the service of the State. It has been estimated that between 1950 and 1966 not less than 50 per cent of the judges and public prosecutors in the Federal German Republic had held similar appointments under the Third Reich; a similar number during those years held important posts in the Foreign Office and the Diplomatic Corps and an even higher percentage of those who held important positions in the Bonn Ministry of the Interior were previously Nazi officials.

The situation as it already existed in 1953 was summarized in a well documented report issued by Editorial Research Reports of Washington, U.S.A.* The report stated that as early as 1947 many Congressmen who had visited West Germany found that the denazification programme was not being carried out efficiently in the American Zone of Occupation, and it gave the following statistics. Out of 3.4 million persons listed as "chargeable cases" 2.5 million were given an amnesty without even appearing before one of the tribunals. Of the remainder "somewhat over 50 per cent stood trial as mere Followers, 11 per cent as Lesser Offenders, 2.3 per cent as Offenders and only 0.17 per

*Editorial Research Reports, Vol. 1, No. 7, by Elizabeth M. Thompson.

cent as Major Offenders". Thus most of those who were tried were only subjected to small fines. Nor was this all. Laws had already been passed by some of the *Lander* which abolished disqualification for public employment of even those who had been classed as Major Offenders. This, the report stated, was one of the main reasons why so many former Nazis had returned to "economic, professional and even political life . . . the increasing tendency is to forgive *and* forget". By 1950 about half the officials in some of the more important Ministries were denazified Nazis who had been reinstated and, Miss Thompson wrote, while "they might not join or encourage a new totalitarian government they would, as before, have little compunction about working for a neo-Nazi Party if one should come to power". This report was written eleven years before the N.P.D. was even formed but, should it ever come to power there is little doubt it would receive such backing from the civil service. When the new West German Foreign Office was formed in 1951, the report continued, Dr. Adenauer admitted, in a statement which he made in the Bundestag, that included in a total staff of 513, there were 134 former Nazi party members and 130 who had been employed in the Foreign Office during the Third Reich. It is significant, in this context, to note that one of the first legislative acts of the Bonn Government was to grant immunity to those who had given false answers to the questionnaire which they had to sign in accordance with the provisions of the Denazification Regulations. This law came into effect on December 31st 1949* and it stated:

> Impunity is granted irrespective of the amount of punishment expected for the offences of withholding personal particulars for political reasons between May 10th 1945 and the coming into force of this new law provided the offender voluntarily withdraws the false statements and gives the necessary information required to his local police station not later than March 31st 1950.

This was the first of many steps taken deliberately to render the denazification programme abortive and to enable many Nazis to get back into the government service.

A number of trials conducted by the International Military Tribunal in Nuremberg after the trial of what were called the

*See *Bundesgesetzblatt*, 1949-50, p. 37.

the major war-criminals, and particularly the trials of Krupp and Flick, clearly proved that many of the leading German industrialists and especially those engaged in the armament industry gave their full support to Hitler as soon as he came to power in 1933. Regardless of this, and contrary to the Potsdam Agreement, firms such as Krupps, Flicks, I. G. Farben, Thyssens and others are, once again, doing business as usual.

At Potsdam the Allies agreed that the concentration of power in the hands of these industrialists should be ended and they took steps to bring this about. By the beginning of 1953, however, it was obvious that the Allies had changed their minds, for in exchange for a pledge by Alfred Krupp to get rid of his coal, steel and iron assets before 1960, all controls were immediately lifted from the other branches of his business which included his shipyards and locomotive plants. It had already been forgotten that in 1948 Krupp had been sentenced to twelve years' imprisonment as a war criminal for "abusing slave labour battalions" which had been placed at his disposal by the S.S.

In opening the case for the prosecution at Krupp's trial General Telford Taylor left the issue in no doubt, for he said: "The individual defendants in this case are not being prosecuted for the sins of others, or because the name of Krupp had acquired over the years a sinister sheen. The men in the dock are not symbols, nor are they charged as representatives of other men. Each defendant is named because the prosecution believe it can prove his personal criminal responsibility."

In the indictment Krupp was charged, *inter alia*, with the following offences: "That he had sought out, requested and recruited foreign workers, prisoners of war and concentration camp inmates from the Third Reich and Satellite government ministries and agencies, from the German military forces, the S.S., the official economic organizations and elsewhere, and had maintained offices in occupied territories and recruited foreign civilians who had been forced, terrorized and misled into his employment. Such recruitments had taken place in Holland, Belgium, France, Poland and Italy." It was also alleged that under the slave labour programme Krupp had employed over 55,000 foreign workers, 18,000 prisoners of war, and more than 5,000 concentration camp inmates. Furthermore, the prosecution brought evidence to prove that Krupp had been directly responsible for looting from factories in countries under German occupation, and was personally concerned in obtaining labour from the concentration camps, and had actually built new factories near the camps at Markstadt and Auschwitz.

This was by no means all. General Telford Taylor called witnesses to prove that on his own premises in Essen Krupp had employed 520 women as slave labour, ranging from 15 to 25 years of age, most of them having been deported from Roumania, Hungary and Czechoslovakia. One of the witnesses gave the following description of what he saw. "Their clothing", he said, "was replaced by a single issue of sack-like grey garments made of burlap and by wooden clogs with fabric tops." In its judgment the Tribunal stated that "torn pieces of blankets were wrapped around their legs and, at times, they had to walk barefoot. There were numerous cases of frozen feet and chilblains. After an air raid on December 31st 1944, the girls had to live in a damp cellar. They were woken each morning at 4 a.m. There were no facilities for washing and they only got one meal a day. Their hair was closely cropped or shaved in the form of a cross. The ill-treatment of these girls was a matter of common knowledge in the firm, and hundreds of them died as a result of all this."

Before Krupp had served even five years of his sentence the United States High Commissioner for Germany, Mr. McCloy, remitted the remainder of the sentence. Krupp was released and all his property restored to him. The move to rearm the Germans had just begun. Germany's armament factories must get moving again. The past must be forgotten.

But Krupp was by no means the only one to get away with it. There were many others including Abs, Ambros, Durrfeld and Frick, all of whom after having been convicted as war criminals now hold high positions in banking and industry.

Dr. Hermann Abs was already in 1938 on the Board of the Deutsche Bank. The directors of the bank, according to documents that are still in existence, through their agents and other business connections, received information regarding Jewish business firms which were to be "Aryanized" and dealt with the confiscated property of such firms. All this took place before the war. During the war the bank expanded its business and the foreign section, under Abs, was made responsible for the "collection of enemy property" which included all Jewish property in the countries which came under German occupation.

According to a report made by the U.S.A. office of Military Government in November 1946, Abs was "the spiritual rector of the infamous Deutsche Bank which combined an unusual concentration of economic power with active participation in the criminal policies of the Nazi Regime . . . Abs exerted all his energy to extend the rule of Germany over Europe." He was not tried by the Allies as a war criminal but he was sentenced by a Yugoslav Court in absentia to fifteen years imprisonment.

Notwithstanding the above, since the occupation of West Germany came to an end Dr. Abs has been again on the Board of the (West) Deutsche Bank, president of the administrative council of the Deutsche Bundesbahn, Chairman of the Badische Anilin and Soda-Fabrik, and on the Board of many other companies. In an article in *Der Spiegel* on November 3rd 1965 dealing with Dr. Abs' great power and influence it was stated that "No ministerial post in Bonn could ever create the range of power and influence which he now has . . . His arm reaches far beyond West Germany. He who ventures a financial undertaking without making use of the Duetsche Bank would feel it very soon . . . A frown from Abs maybe the decisive factor regarding credits of millions or a managerial career."

Otto Ambros started the I. G. Farben factory in Auschwitz. Before choosing the site he considered several others but eventually decided on Auschwitz because, according to the evidence which he gave before the Nuremberg Tribunal, "there was an adequate supply of water in addition to brine and coal". Furthermore, the man-power question in this region was also favourable because of the high population density. As director of the I. G. Farben works in Auschwitz ,Monowitz Ambros was the immediate superior of Dr. Durrfeld and was kept informed by him of all that was going on. The main source of labour was, of course, the local concentration camp and the S.S. saw to it that I. G. Farben were supplied with workers. This was arranged in co-operation with the R.S.H.A. and, more directly, with the Commandant of the camp. It was essential that the labour supplied should be fully fit, so when the camp inmates employed there became unfit because of the conditions in which they worked, which happened very frequently, substitutes were always available and the others were sent back to the camp from which they had come and were duly exterminated.

In 1948 the U.S. Military Tribunal in Nuremberg sentenced Ambros to eight years imprisonment for the crimes committed by him in Auschwitz against the Jews. His conviction as a war-criminal, however, appears to have been forgotten for, since his release, he has been appointed to the Board of many of the leading chemical enterprises and other companies, including the Scholven-Chemie A.G., the Gelsenkirchen-Buer and the Telefunken A.G.

Dr. Durrfeld, already mentioned above, was works manager under Ambros at the I. G. Farben works in Auschwitz from 1943 to 1945 and it was he who personally conducted the negotiations on the mass employment of concentration camp victims at these works, on instructions from Ambros, with Obergruppenführer Wolf in Berlin. When the workers were no longer fit for work they were sent back to the camp to be gassed with Zyklon B and at least 300,000 of those who had been employed in the I. G. Farben works met their death in this way. His efforts on behalf of the company were greatly appreciated and on December 14th 1944 Ambros asked for Durrfeld's salary to be increased on the grounds that he had "given special service in the construction of the Auschwitz works". He was sentenced after the war by an American Military Tribunal to eight years imprisonment for committing "war crimes and crimes against humanity", but was released before the expiry of his sentence and immediately re-employed by I. G. Farben and appointed to the Board of Scholven-Chemie, A.G.

Friedrick Flick was an industrialist with considerable influence during the Third Reich. He was a member of "Himmler's circle of friends" and hand in glove with Göring with regard to what was known as the Organization Programme. At his trial by an American Military Tribunal in 1947 the prosecutor stated, in his closing speech, that the evidence had proved that the accused personally participated in this Aryanization—a Nazi euphemism for depriving Jews of all their property and other assets—from which he obtained enormous profits both for himself and for his companies. In addition to this he employed more than 50,000 slave labourers, prisoners of war, and concentration camp inmates, many thousands of whom died from overwork and malnutrition. The Tribunal sentenced him to seven years imprisonment but, like Krupp, he was released before expiry of his sentence. He is now, once again, a great power in West German industry and his companies have an important share in the production of tanks, missiles, explosives and all kinds of ammunition. He also has a close relationship with some of the more influential members of the Christian Democrats.

It is extremely unlikely that any of those mentioned above, who gave active support to Hitler without, apparently, any scruples or any misgivings would not once again jump on the band waggon should they think it was in their interest so to do. And there are hundreds more like them.

But it is not only in the civil service and big business that ex-Nazis have been coming to the fore. The judiciary has also had its fair share of them. Shortly after Hitler came into power special courts were set up to deal with so-called political offenders and their task was "to extirpate the opponents of the Third Reich, particularly Communists and Social Democrats". That they had this special jurisdiction was confirmed in a judgment of the German Supreme Court on November 9th 1938. After the outbreak of war they were set up in all the countries occupied by the Nazis and, according to the available statistics passed not less than 50,000 death sentences. They were euphemistically known as the Peoples' Court since all the crimes which Hitler committed were done "in the name of the German people".

After the war a Lawyer's Trial was held in Germany by an American Tribunal and in its judgment the following passage can be read: "The essence of the charge in this case is that the law, the decrees and the corrupt and perverted national-socialist system of law, of itself constituted war crimes and crimes against humanity, and that those taking part in the enactment or application of these laws are criminally involved as accessories in those crimes . . . In brief, the charge is one of conscious participation in a system of cruelty and injustice, organized by the government and extending over the whole country, offending against the laws of war and humanity, and committed in the name of the law, by the authority of the Ministry of Justice, and with the help of the courts. The robes of the judge concealed the hand of the murderer."

It was for this reason, therefore, that in pursuance of the Potsdam Agreement the Allied Control Council laid it down that "in order to reform the German system of justice all ex-members of the Nazi party who took any active part in its work, and all others who had any direct part in the system of punishment applied by the Hitler regime must be removed from their posts as judges and prosecutors, and no such persons must be permitted to take up such posts".

In West Germany, however, this was, unfortunately, never fully implemented, or anywhere near it, and from the very early days of the new Federal Republic a large number of prominent Nazis who had held appointments in the judicial branch of the Nazi Government were allowed to remain, and even when much later severe public criticism of this arose in Germany these men were not dismissed but were given an opportunity of an early retirement with pension. Such criticism was entirely justified and there are still some ex-Nazis holding judicial appointments and they have been allowed to sit in judgment in cases involving Nazis crimes.

In 1959 this matter was raised by Herr Erich Ollenhauer, leader of the Social Democrats (S.D.P.) who wrote: "The basic law which is our constitution has established an ethical code of decency and conduct which would allow our law courts to deal with any offenders. There is, however, the question whether the judges presiding over these courts are able or willing to apply these laws. This brings us to the question of the removal of officials. Our party has for years clamoured for the removal of some former Nazi officials who have sought and found shelter also in the highest government positions. This is an eminently political task, and *some* progress has been made." It is to be hoped, now, that there is a coalition between the S.P.D. and the C.D.U., that this fight by the Social Democrats will still continue.

To illustrate the foundation for Herr Ollenhauer's apprehension the American Jewish Congress's Commission on International Affairs, in a report published in 1959,* gave some striking examples.

* *The German Dilemma.*

(1) A court in Duisburg which was trying a Nazi official for having ordered the burning of a synagogue in Mulheim during the Crystal Night pogrom* dismissed the charge on the slender pretext that as the synagogue had been sold before it was set on fire it was no longer "a house of worship".

(2) In Wiesbaden another court acquitted five high officials of the Ministry of Justice although there was ample evidence to prove that they had been responsible for the death of 2,000 inmates of a concentration camp.

(3) A third court, in Hamburg, ruled that the concentration camps were a necessary institution.

Decisions like the above were not only criticized by many ordinary Germans. The former President of the Federal Republic, Theodor Heuss, said that there had been "some unfortunate Court decisions, causing distress to the State itself, which by law recognizes the 'independence' of the courts".

It also seems rather unfortunate that the present Supreme Commander of N.A.T.O. Forces in Europe, General Graf von Kielmansegg, should have been selected to take up this appointment, whatever his military achievements may be, for he wrote a book which was published in 1941 by the publishing house, Die Wehrmact entitled *Panzer Zwischen Warshau und Atlantik* (Tanks between Warsaw and the Atlantic) describing his experiences during the invasion of Poland in September 1939 when he was a general staff officer of the First Panzer Division. The following are extracts from his book.

> In the village of Polichno we also introduced, for the first time, a method of ensuring a night's rest which later became a regulation and stood the test very well. All the *surviving*† inhabitants of the village were herded together in a big yard and locked up for the night . . .
>
> It was incredible in Wistitski. It was impossible to have quarters there. The houses were caked with filth, the air could hardly be

*This was November 9th 1938, during what is generally known as the "Week of Broken Glass". On this night demonstrations took place throughout the Reich in protest against the attempted assassination of Von Roth, Secretary in the German Embassy in Paris. According to a report sent by Reinhardt Heydrich to Hermann Göring, 191 synagogues and 171 Jewish apartment houses were set on fire, and 815 shops were looted. Afterwards, 20,000 Jews were taken into "protective custody", and 9,815 of them sent to the concentration camp at Buchenwald.

†The italics are mine.

breathed. That was accounted for when one saw that almost all the inhabitants were Jewish. We hardly believed it possible that so many of these types which had been described in *Der Sturmer** but have not actually been seen in Germany could be found in such numbers, and to such a degree of perfection in the negative sense, in Poland.

There was a time, many years ago but, perhaps, not in these days, when the expression of such views in print would have been an immediate disqualification for high command in any military force which is partly subsidized by Jewish tax-payers and in which some Jews even happen to be serving. It should not be forgotten that the General is not merely commanding German troops and that N.A.T.O. comprises large contingents from many of the countries which were occupied by the Nazis during the war to whom, it would be reasonable to suppose, such sentiments would not be palatable.

In this chapter certain factual statements have been made about a number of Germans now holding important and influential positions. It is not suggested that they were all war criminals, some of them were not, yet many of them were tried after 1945 for war crimes and crimes against humanity, in accordance with the provisions of the Nuremberg Charter. For example, as Mr. Ivor Montagu has written in his book *Germany's new Nazis*, "It may be that Kiesinger really misjudged the course of history and thought that he could influence for good such a monstrosity as the Nazi Party; that von Kilmansegg is not really the character that he appears in these quotations from his book: that in twenty years he has had time to change." What is certain, however, is that it is too soon to be sure of this and only time will tell, but with such people at the helm and having regard to Germany's past history it is not surprising that some people, including many Germans, make certain reservations.

One reason for this is the obstruction which many writers receive when they try to get information from the official archives about the careers of such people. They are politely told that such information is not available in certain circumstances.

*An anti-Semitic periodical produced by Julius Streicher. See *The Scourge of the Swastika*.

What happened to one application of this kind is rather revealing.

An English businessman, a Mr. Horten, who has been making frequent visits to Germany since 1960 on behalf of large U.S. and U.K. engineering groups which have interests in Germany was disturbed to find, having the opportunity of studying post-war Germany at close quarters, that what he calls "the more extreme forms of the German way of life and philosophy" are still present in such organizations as the police, the armed forces, films, theatres, schools, industry, politics and government. Having decided to write a book on this subject he sent a letter to the Foreign Office in London on December 13th 1966 asking whether arrangements could be made for him to have access to the Berlin Document Center*. He was then told to write personally to the Director of the Center and this he did. A couple of months later the Director sent Mr. Horten a number of forms to fill in, giving particulars of the persons about whom he wished to get information. A few weeks later he was surprised to receive the following letter signed by the Director herself.

> Dear Mr. Horten,
>
> I have received your letter of August 27th with the enclosed check forms. A review of the previous correspondence has revealed that one rather essential factor has been overlooked in your case. Your proposed book deals with post-war Germany.
>
> It has always been the policy of the Berlin Document Center to grant access to its biographical files only to scholars conducting research on the history of the Third Reich. I regret that this restriction was not pointed out to you before.
>
> In order that the Foreign Office may know of the decision in your case, I am forwarding this letter to you through government channels.
>
> Sincerely Yours,
> Lucile Petterson
> Director
> Berlin Document Center.

The Director's reply to Mr. Horten was duly received by him with a covering letter from the Foreign Office Librarian and Keeper of the Papers. In it the Librarian stated that the

*The Berlin Document Center is run by the Mission of the United States of America in West Berlin.

Director had "only just realized", that Mr. Horten's application was to be given access to files "relating to present day West German politicians and industrialists". This was rather strange, having regard to the fact that, in his original letter of December 13th 1966, which had been forwarded to the Berlin Document Center by the Foreign Office Librarian, Mr. Horten had clearly stated that he was "writing a serious book on post-war Germany". The Librarian ended his letter by offering his regrets and those of the British Office of Military Government in Berlin that they had not realized sooner the difficulty created by the fact that Mr. Horten's proposed book was on "a *post-war* subject".

This official secretiveness is rather ominous and even if the reason for it is not, as it would apparently seem to be, an unwillingness to reveal the past it is bound to raise the suspicion that it is. The excuse which is always given by the Bonn Government, as has already been pointed out, is that the infiltration of former Nazis into important positions in public life was inevitable in order to rebuild Germany quickly so that she could again play an important role in western Europe. That may well be so, but there are many Germans who feel that a more gradual recovery would have been less dangerous. The future of democracy in Western Germany would be safer if there were not so many former Nazis in high places.

Although Dr. Adenauer strenuously defended his appointment of Dr. Globke to such an important post to the bitter end and told the Bundestag that a Foreign Office could not be rebuilt with amateurs he was not so successful in the case of Dr. Oberlander who held the post of Minister for Expellees in his Cabinet. Oberlander had been an officer in the S.S. and a member of the Abwehr. According to an article which appeared in *Die Zeit* on October 9th 1959 he was an expert "in the treatment of other races" and held the post of political officer in an S.S. unit which entered Lemberg in Poland and was responsible for the murder of 7,000 civilians in two days. He admitted that he was in Lemberg at that time but said that while he was there "not a single shot was fired". About the same time as this article appeared there was so much public criticism of his being a member of the Adenauer Cabinet that he had to resign. Nevertheless, while he was Minister, he was responsible for appointing many former prominent Nazis, to posts in the Ministry, and many of them are still there.

Another notable Nazi, who became head of the Information Office for the Marshall Plan in 1950, was Dr. Sonnenhal. He joined the N.S.D.A.P. three years before Hitler became Chancellor and, according to the *Frankfurter Rundschau*, said that to have served in the S.S. "had been an honour".

This list could continue almost endlessly. At the present time there are many former Nazis in all the government offices of the Federal Government, in the judiciary, in the schools and in some universities, in banking, in industrial management and even in the Bundeswehr, and the situation will not change greatly for at least ten years. Should democracy in the Federal Republic not stand the test of time, and many Germans fear that it may not, many of these men would continue to serve another totalitarian government just as most of their forbears did when the Weimar Republic collapsed and was superseded by the Third Reich.

CHAPTER FIVE

Glorifying the Führer

One of the most significant aspects of the possible danger within the next few years of the resurgence of nationalism in the Federal Republic gaining impetus and becoming more popular with a new generation which has no personal connection with the Third Reich is the enormous spate of literature of one form or another glorifying Hitler and covering up the terrible events which took place in Germany and throughout occupied Europe during those twelve years. They include the memoirs of German generals and diplomats, novels, and other books, pamphlets and periodicals justifying the war, making excuses for having lost it, criticising the trial of war criminals, and making allegations of the ill-treatment of German prisoners of war and of the inmates of the Allied internment camps.

Although most of the memoirs written by distinguished German generals blame Hitler's amateur interference for the loss of the war they make no other criticism of him. Most of these professional soldiers also deny emphatically any knowledge of what went on in the concentration camps and of the appalling crimes which were committed by some of the Einsatzgruppen* under their very noses. General Guderian, for example, has stated that he "became aware of the inhumanities perpetrated in such camps only after the collapse. The system of keeping the secret of the concentration camps methods must be called nothing short of ingenious", and he dismissed the rumours that spread around about the Final Solution as "atrocity stories against the Germans set afoot with Jewish thoroughness".

It is difficult to believe these protestations of total ignorance. The concentration camp of Belsen, to give only one example,

*Special Action Groups.

was just outside the village of Bergen-Belsen and many of the villagers were employed there during the day and returned home every evening. During this time they must have had contact with many soldiers who were at home on leave and it is unlikely that they never spoke of what they had seen in the camp. Is it reasonable to suppose that these stories were never repeated? Furthermore, Germans who, during the war, indulged in careless talk used to be told—"You had better be careful or you'll go up the chimney". To what could that refer but the concentration camp crematoriums? The concentration camp system had been in existence in Germany for several years before the war, and many Germans had had friends and relations in the camps some of whom were subsequently released.

Field-Marshal von Manstein, who wrote a book of reminiscences entitled *Lost Victories*, also stated that he was unaware of the mass extermination of many thousands of Jews by shooting, hanging, gassing and drowning carried out by Einsatzgruppe D, attached to the Eleventh Army which he commanded in Russia between September 1941 and February 1943. There is, however, ample evidence that he did know what went on. When his Army was operating in the Ukraine orders were given by Himmler that the Jews were to be "liquidated". The existence of these orders and their execution were known to the Army Commander and an order was issued by the Eleventh Army that no liquidation must take place within 200 kilometres of Army Headquarters. Furthermore, only a few days after the invasion of Russia had begun von Manstein issued a directive for the behaviour of the troops in Russia as an appendix to one of his operation orders. It urged them to take ruthless measures against "Bolshevik instigators, francs-tireurs, saboteurs, and *Jews*".

The Field-Marshal had known exactly what kind of war it was going to be ever since the conference which Hitler had held three months before Russia was invaded. The Führer told the generals who attended the conference, and von Manstein was one of them, that it would differ from the war in the West and chivalry and military honour would have no place in it.

The memoirs of von Ribbentrop, who had been the German Ambassador in London before the war was entitled *Between*

London and Moscow. As might be expected it not only vindicated Hitler, it almost deified him. He was, according to von Ribbentrop, "a man of overwhelming intelligence with a staggering gift of comprehension, who in his entire life had only one goal, to serve the German people". But the former Minister of Foreign Affairs omitted to say that in order to do this he deliberately murdered millions of innocent civilians. These memoirs were reprinted several times and hundreds of thousands of copies must have been sold and were undoubtedly read. Editions were also published in Great Britain, France, Italy and Spain. To the neo-Nazis it came as a god-send and the newspaper of the Deutsches Reich Partei called it a "veritable treasure-trove" and "a work of source materials which scholarship will not be able to ignore and which will force it to abandon the thesis of Germany's sole guilt in having provoked World War II".

In 1952 Rudolf Hess once again came into the picture when a volume of his letters were published under the title *England, Nuremberg, Spandau* to which his wife wrote an introductory chapter. This proved to be such a success, that having reached its twenty-third edition in less than four years, an attempt was made by a group of authors and publishers to get the book banned on the grounds that it was subversive of democracy, for in whatever way he might have changed his mind he was still of the opinion that his beloved Führer was "the greatest son the German people have produced in their thousand years of history".

Hess's book must have influenced the minds of many of the thousands who read it, including some of his former enemies abroad who read the English edition, for there was considerable sympathy for him having regard to the fact that when he made his unsuccessful attempt to end the war by flying to Scotland it was thought that he had seen the error of his ways. At his trial by the International Military Tribunal in Nuremberg, however, he made it clear that he had done no such thing. In his final speech on that occasion he said, "I regret nothing. If I had to start all over again, I would act again as I acted before, even if I knew that at the end a burning pyre was waiting for my death at the stakes". As he made it clear in some of the letters which he had written while he was serving his sentence in Spandau that he was still of this opinion, the decision of the court which decided that the book should not be banned provides further evidence of the bias of many German courts in favour of the Nazis. In its judgment the court stated that "conceivably some unregenerate National Socialist might find in such books confirmation for their mistaken political views" but they took the view "that the letters did not contribute to the promotion of nationalism". There was another series of publications, called the Dime Novels, which were on sale at a cheap price at all the large booksellers and railway station bookstands and must also have been read by many thousands of Germans, and, particularly, by the younger generation. The whole object of these books was to glamourize Hitler as a private individual by giving him a homely image. No mention was made of his political ideas or objectives. Everything unpleasant was purposely omitted and the Nazis' crimes carefully concealed.

In addition to the reminiscences of famous generals, leading diplomats, and leaders of the Nazi Party many family memoirs have also been published since the end of the war. One of these was written by the wife of Baldur von Shirach, leader of the Hitler Jugend, who was, a year ago, released from Spandau leaving Rudolf Hess as the only major war criminal still in custody. Although Frau von Shirach's book makes no excuses for the Third Reich it is subtle propaganda of a dangerous kind for, like the Dime Novels, it deals mainly with the personal and private lives of her husband and some of his Nazi colleagues. As Kurt Tauber wrote in his book, "while in no sense wishing to glorify the 'splendour' of the past, the very accent on the personal, the homely, the anecdotal, conveys the impression that the Nazi leaders were really estimable fellows who by pure chance got involved in unpleasant things".

Some of the most popular post-war books, however, have a much more direct objective, namely the glorification of Hitler as Germany's Führer, the justification of the Nazi terror and counter charges against the Allies.

A few examples are given below:

(1) In 1955 a biography of Hitler appeared under the pseudonym of W. von Asenbach, the real identity of whom is not definitely known. The following extract is typical of the whole book.

> The propaganda drums are still being beaten today because of those Jews who were *allegedly** executed in the camps on Hitler's orders. In this connection the most quoted figure of six million is pure fantasy; was it, perhaps, not true that the Jews had also to be recognized in the Second World War as a belligerent party and treated accordingly?
>
> Jewry appears not only everywhere as the driving force of implacableness, and of hatred . . . but as the suppliers of masses of spies and the financiers and organizers of the guerilla war against the German Army . . . The world has the Jews to thank not only for the global spread of the war but also for the deaths of millions of soldiers, old men, women and children.

A few months after the publication of this book it was banned on the fiat of the Federal Attorney-General but it continued to be sold by underground means in the same way as the provisions of the British Race Relations Act were, until recently, evaded by selling subversive and pro-Nazi literature published by the "Greater Britain Movement" only to persons who became members of the Viking Book Club by paying an entrance fee of sixpence.

(2) A similar book entitled *Stalingrad, the Lost Victory*, which among other things blamed the "army traitors" for the German defeat at Stalingrad also had large sales although its author was later prosecuted for publishing "subversive materials", sentenced to two years imprisonment and prohibited from writing any further books for five years.

(3) General Remer, leader of the S.R.P. wrote a book about the attempt on Hitler's life on July 20th 1944 which stated that the conspiracy was not merely directed against Hitler and National Socialism but against Germany itself, an accusation which was repeated almost word for word in another book by Rudel on the subject of the old "stab-in-the-back" legend.

(4) An attempt to divest Germany of any responsibility for the Second World War was also made in 1954, by no means for the first time, by the publication in pamphlet form of a speech made by Dietrich Klegges, the former Nazi Minister President of Brunswick. "The Second World War", he said, "was never an aggressive war: it was a war of liberation to which the German people had roused themselves to throw off the slave chains

*The italics are mine.

which had been wrought at Versailles, to regain the territories in all parts of the world which had been unjustly torn from us, to occupy, again, as a great and free nation the place among the world powers which is its due . . . And how is it with war crimes? It is certain that these misdeeds occurred not only on our side. Was not the unrestrained bombing of the defenceless civilian population a war crime . . . and was not that which the victorious powers did to the German people during and after the occupation, horror upon horror, doubly detestable because it was done to defenceless people?"

The pamphlet contained many other accusations against the Allies and justification of Hitler's tyranny. The potential danger of this kind of propaganda is that the young people who are unaware of the true facts may believe it, whereas those who did know the facts are only too glad to hear it. "There you are", they say to their children, "What did we tell you? We were not the aggressors. We went to war to defend our country, and have we not always told you that the stories about the gassing of millions of Jews and the massacre of innocent civilians is a load of rubbish."

(5) An even more outspoken denial of German guilt was made in a book published in 1953 entitled *We acquit Hitler*, which dealt specifically with the Final Solution and quoted an imaginary speech by Hitler. "One always hears talk of five to six million Jews* despite the fact that this figure neither corresponds to reality nor was ever proved. The number of Jews I was able to get hold of was between one and two million. At best I can be held responsible for the death of one and a half million Jews . . . In this war all participating people have had to pay their levy of blood. The losses of these people far exceeds that of the Jewish people. If the world considers that an injustice it must also do so in the case of all German civilians who lost their lives through the war, more or less by premeditation and especially after the collapse of Germany . . . For me it was a matter of maintenance of the German people, and for that every means were justified!"

(6) Other books portrayed Hitler as the liberator from the yoke of Versailles, and a statesman devoted to peace. "Will

*The estimated number given by the prosecution at the Nuremberg trial of major war criminals was 6,000,000. The real number will never be known but it is safe to say that it is over 5,000,000.

Germans one day think big enough to place Hitler's statue in front of the ruins of the Reichstag in Berlin?" asked the former deputy Reich press chief, Herr Helmuth Sündermann. Whether they will ever do so for the reason Herr Sündermann wants it to be there, it is too early to say. Nevertheless it would be a fitting memorial to the man who ruled Germany as a dictator for nearly twelve years.

Of the other books, and their name is legion, written for the sole purpose of minimizing the crimes committed by the Nazis, a large percentage dealt with the Jewish problem which Adolf von Thadden has said "no longer exists in Germany today because there are only 30,000 of them left and most of them are old". The Final Solution still remains the permanent chip on the German's shoulder. It is because it was the greatest crime in world history that it has to be totally denied, reduced to more reasonable proportions or blatantly justified.

The following extracts from some of these books are typical of them all.

"Supposedly they (the Jews) were systematically tortured. This is totally untrue. At the worst one or two prisoners might have been slapped in the face for their brazen demeanour". This assessment of what happened to the Jews under Hitler is not surprising having regard to the fact that it was written by Julius Lippert who, twenty years before when he was the Mayor of Berlin, made a speech in which he said, "To me the Jew is not a human being. Look at him: thick lips, greedy eyes, dishonest by acquired property . . . what animal should suffer the unreasonable imputation of being compared with them?"

"There were until the war between 500,000 and 600,000 Jews in Germany. If 60,000 of them had been killed it would remain a horrible figure. What happened outside of Germany has to be added to this number and in Switzerland a 'possible' figure of one and a half million has been mentioned, but German statistics cannot put the number above 350,000." This was Hans Grimm's way of exposing some of the accusations made against Hitler which "had to be based on forgeries, one of which was the invention of the six million murdered Jews".

In another book, written by Peter Kleist, entitled *Between Hitler and Stalin*, the threadbare accusation that the Jews are responsible for all the ills of the world was brought up to date.

"The great international press agencies", Kleist wrote, "very often in the hands of Jews or working with Jewish correspondents, launched a propaganda campaign against Germany which in point of ingenuity rivalled that of 1914-18 and which enormously exaggerated events in the Third Reich. The rape of Jewish girls, the put-out eyes and chopped off hands, everything was again trotted out and supplied Hitler with proof for his preconceived opinion of a world conspiracy of Jewry against awakening Germany." Later, when dealing with the concentration camps, Kleist compared the Gestapo reign of terror in Germany itself to Defence Regulation 18 B which was used during the war by the British Government to detain without trial persons who were considered to be dangerous for reasons of security.*

The last category of this spate of pro-Nazi propaganda includes a number of publications dealing with alleged war crimes committed by the Allies and the iniquity of the trials of German war criminals. Exactly what effect all these denials, excuses and counter-charges are having on the millions who read them cannot be estimated, but the very fact that they continue to be made is evidence of the attempts being made to subvert democratic government in the Federal Republic and this should not be ignored. The Hitler-like speeches made by von Thadden at the N.P.D.'s conference in Hanover in November 1967 make this abundantly clear.

*This was not the first time the Germans had manufactured similar propaganda against the British. The first occasion was during the South Africa war when Britain was accused of the murder and ill-treatment of thousands of Boer men, women and children in the internment camps. These accusations were repeated after the defeat of Germany in 1945 when the Germans said that it was the British who had first "started the concentration camps". As the true facts are not generally known they are given in Appendix III.

CHAPTER SIX

The N.P.D.

THE EARLIER chapters of this book have shown that ever since the unconditional surrender of the Germans in 1945 there has remained an undercurrent of Nazism in Western Germany, even during the days when it was occupied by the Allies, and from time to time disturbing signs of what is generally called Neo-Nazism. If this evidence were to be put in the form of a graph it would be seen to have remained at roughly the same level until the end of the 1950s, when it rose suddenly on the alarming outbreak of anti-Semitism, which has been described in Chapter III, and then to have descended gradually until the autumn of 1966 when the N.P.D. suddenly came into the limelight by obtaining about 8 per cent of the votes in the *Land* elections in Hesse which it followed up shortly afterwards by striking successes in Bavaria and Niedersachsen.

Eight per cent of the votes in an election may seem to many to be a drop in the ocean, but even the Federal Minister of the Interior, Herr Lucke, described these successes as an "alarm signal" that should not be ignored. It is most important that the possibility of the N.P.D. becoming a power in the Federal German Republic after the next Bundestag elections should not be underestimated for what is apparent at the moment is like the top of an iceberg. It is what is below the surface which could cause the damage, for although there is no mention of Hitler in the Party's Manifesto, neither praise nor blame, some of its principles and slogans are very similar to his. The denial of war guilt, praise of German militarism, and the German's right to territorial expansion—the old doctrine of *Lebensraum.*

Anti-Semitism is not part of the N.P.D.'s stated policy, as it was with the Nazis, but they are not troubled with what Hitler called the Jewish Question for the simple reason, as von

Thadden has stated publicly on more than one occasion, "there are only 30,000 of them left and most of them are old and keep quiet".

The tip of the iceberg, however, may still appear innocuous to those who wish to forget Germany's past history or are ignorant of it, and the Party's leaders have left no stone unturned to make it appear harmless. As has been said by an experienced observer of right wing extremists in the Federal Republic, "The people who are running the N.P.D. are smart. They know exactly how far they can go legally and they never say anything that can be proved to be out-and-out Nazi. Their technique is subtle. They do not publicly praise Hitler but recently thousands of the Party's members attended the funeral of a Nazi general who had been convicted of ordering the massacre of American prisoners of war."

But what the N.P.D. is really like has been vividly revealed in an article written by Mr. Ivor Montagu* describing a meeting which took place in a typical German Bierhalle in Harburg, which is close to Hamburg, towards the end of November 1966. This meeting, according to Mr. Montagu, was not a mass meeting or one characterized by any sort of election excitement or frenzy (it was held shortly after the Hesse successes and there was, therefore, some cause for jubilation); it was just such a meeting as is being held by the N.P.D. week-in and week-out up and down the Federal Republic, concentrating especially, of course, on the areas scheduled for coming elections. Extracts from Mr. Montagu's article, which was entitled, "Night out in a beer-hall", are set-out below.

> The scene is a beer-hall. In Germany many taverns have attached to them a big hall for meetings with a thousand seats or more. This is a large one but its seating is limited by a cross table at one end and five rows of tables with seats on each side running down the length of the hall. The hall is filling up. There are getting on for 200 persons present. Some of them are fat with thick necks. about one third of them are under 25. No more than a fifth of them are women . . . The posters advertising the meeting have been done in red Nazi style:† the only difference being that,

*Originally published in *The Morning Star* and reproduced in *Germany's New Nazis*, Panther Books.

†Similar posters can be seen today all over Germany.

instead of the swastika, in the circle is "N.P.D."* The meeting starts late. The Chairman explains that the S.D.P. (Social Democrats) tried to prevent their meeting . . . and he complains, "Where is order if a democratic party cannot carry through its activity unless protected by the police".

The next speaker says he knows the new government. "I resigned from the National Socialist Party on the same day that Chancellor Kiesinger says he did" (laughter and applause). "And as for Herr Brandt, the Vice-Chancellor, I sat beside him on the same school bench. He may have changed his name—and his nationality—but not his nature." Then came the orator of the evening. He is slim, good looking, well poised with hair slightly greying to emphasize his authority. He is a historian, sacked (he claims) from school teaching for telling the truth which the other three parties† appointed by the Allies after their conquest, and with leaders chosen by the Allies, are in a common conspiracy to hide . . . His whole lecture is a repudiation of German guilt—guilt for the war, guilt for war crimes—and a call to Germans to recover respect and to insist upon *Gleichberechtigung*, equality of rights, as the solution to their problems.

Like Hitler, he begins with Versailles, "Lloyd George said 'If we take the guilt out of Versailles, the whole will fall down!'"

Churchill and Roosevelt are particular targets. "Tragic that U.S. President should decide matters without the slightest knowledge of history." He was just as ignorant as President Wilson in his day. Roosevelt had not the least idea of the nature of Bolshevism: he was so stupid he could not write his own speeches and was surrounded by Communists spies such as Harry Hopkins and the President of the World Bank. All three parties in Britain were agreed on maintaining the balance of power. Churchill said that the Polish guarantee was given for no other reason, and meant the death of millions. But were the British public told this? No, they had no choice. The last democrat in England was Neville Chamberlain and he was told he would be overthrown if he did not go to war. In the U.S. Roosevelt said: "Vote for the Democrats who kept you out of war. No American boy will be sent to Europe". His opponent, Wendell Wilkie said: "Roosevelt is taking you into war. The Republicans will stop it".

Now the U.S. Senate had frankly admitted that Roosevelt deceived the people. But when Wendell Wilkie was asked about his attitude and reminded of his promises he told journalists: "That was just electioneering".

*Nationalische Partei Democratische.

†i.e. The Christian Democrats, The Social Democrats and the Free Democrats.

That is what they call democracy, but it didn't give you any chance, you can't have men sued for breaking election promises.
Did they ever disclose that after the Polish campaign Hitler offered the British immediate peace without a single condition? . . .

"Not one spokesman of the three big German parties has stood up to say that what the Allies have forced us to write in our history books is false".

The greatest cheers were received for the exculpation for war crimes. "They say six to ten million Jews were killed. Scientific studies show that it was not so many. Whether it was hundreds or thousands does not matter so much: What does matter is that not all crimes were on one side. Many were worse on the other side, and they never tell you which came first!" A storm of applause.

"We have paid 43 milliards in compensation to Israel. Three or four milliards would have been quite enough . . . we are not here to clear the death of Hitler or the dead S.S. but to stop the slander of the German people. Tens of thousands were made to sit in prison and see all the best fruits going to those who opposed the German people . . ."

"Our party has come along just in time . . . The 700,000 votes we have gained in the *Land* elections prove that we shall gain hundreds of thousands more."

The orator sat down, the chairman thanked him and then, declaring that democratic discussion was welcome, invited questions or five minutes speeches from the floor. Three young men in turn, an older man—a former concentration camp victim—and a girl, seized their opportunity and came up on to the platform.

They spoke clearly and economically, challenging the facts stated, but saying they were chiefly interested not in ancient history but in knowing the N.P.D.'s policies for the present, and how it intended to carry them out . . . The chief speaker replied urbanely, if condescendingly, for the most part answering that before the young people presumed to argue about such things they should study the works of older people and read his books. As for the Party's policies, he said, they could not be repeated at every meeting: he would send them free a copy of the party paper.

But the supporters grew restive. They found such restraint distasteful. Their shouts and interruptions grew more and more frequent. When the concentration camp victim had spoken a dried-up man seized the microphone and shouted venemously: "We know you, and we have noted every word you said."

When a young man in glasses said firmly, "As for Brandt, what he did was a thousand times better than your heroes. He fought not against Germany but against those who shamed and betrayed it", all manners vanished. People shouted, banged the tables, rose in their seats. Amid the hubbub the squat N.P.D. man got again to the microphone and screamed in a frenzy: "We Germans have a guilt complex! Look at the judges who condemn us! I agree we killed one million Jews. But the English in South Africa killed 280,000 in their own concentration camps*—for gold, not politics! I saw the monument to it. And they tied women to cannons and shot them to pieces. As for the U.S. everyone knows that there they keep knocking niggers dead! We demand equal for equal." The hall rang with applause.

Soon after, the orator having excused the excitement of the crowd as a natural reaction to the slander on the whole German army, the chairman repeated the assertion they were all good democrats and appealed for funds before the closing.

We had seen the neo-Nazis on their best behaviour.

On their best behaviour perhaps, but Mr. Montagu's account of this meeting reveals enough of what is really under the surface to make one very suspicious about the Party's insistence that it is democratic. The British Foreign Secretary, Mr. George Brown, has said that Germany's leaders are all good democrats. Now that Herr Kiesinger has become Chancellor it would seem that this is a somewhat premature assessment. However the next few years will tell.

The new Chancellor joined the Nazi party in 1933 when he was an attorney and employed as a "Scientific assistant" in the Foreign Office and within quite a short time he was promoted to be deputy chief of the radio policy department. This department according to Hitler's decree of September 8th 1939 was responsible for the "implementation of the Directives and instructions for the foreign propaganda of the German broadcasting network" issued by the Foreign Minister. He was, in this capacity, also closely in liaison with Goebbel's Ministry of Propaganda. This he has admitted but he said that it would be quite wrong, as some people have done, to describe him as an important link between Ribbentrop and Goebbels.

In February 1967 Chancellor Kiesinger was interviewed by Alfred Wolfmann, an Israeli journalist on a Tel-Aviv newspaper

*See Appendix III.

Yedioth Achronoth, an interview which was later published in *Vorwarts*. He told Wolfmann that he only joined the Nazis because he and his friends in the Catholic Vereinigung thought that "one should try to influence", but after the Röhm Putsch of 1934 he "realized that nothing sensible could be done". Nevertheless he stayed on although he "never believed in Nazism but thought it ought to be moderated". Wolfmann asked him whether it was not possible to resign from the Party to which he replied, "Yes, in 1934-35 one could have done it. But one did not foresee the course of history". There can have been few active members of the N.S.D.A.P. who, in 1935, did not have a pretty good idea where Hitler was leading them, and the N.P.D. can be fairly confident that while Kiesinger remains Chancellor it is unlikely that they will get into trouble.

It was reported in the *National-Zeitung* of June 17th 1966 that to "the question asked him at a press conference in Stuttgart as to whether he supports banning the N.P.D. he replied that he does not think much of applying executive measures in combating new emerging parties which are said to possess nationalistic tendencies".

It is little wonder that his appointment as Chancellor was not unwelcome to the N.P.D. for there can be few, if any, of the Party's Basic Principles, as set out in the Manifesto, with which he is not in agreement even though he may be careful not to admit it in public. As Carlo Schmid was told by his party some years ago when he dared to suggest that the reunification of Germany was clearly unattainable in the foreseable future, "You may think it but you must not say it".

The N.P.D. was formed in November 1964 so that members of three other small parties could merge and by so doing have an opportunity of obtaining the 5 per cent minimum of the total number of votes cast in the September Bundestag elections which must be obtained in order to be represented in the Federal Parliament. The new Party represented a merger of elements from these three ultra-right wing groups, The Deutsche Partei, the Gesamdeutsche Partei and the Deutsche Reichs-Partei* including the so-called "expellees" and refugees from East

*Not to be confused with The Deutsche Rechts-Partei (1946–59), also known by the initials D.R.P.

Germany, the German Democratic Republic, as it is called, of whom there are about eight million. Until the autumn of 1966 this five per cent had never been achieved and on the first occasion when the N.P.D. contested an election it polled a mere 2.1 per cent of the total vote (660,000), although in some areas which had always been Nazi strongholds they did much better, obtaining from seven to fifteen per cent in some cities, expecially in Bavaria.

The founder of the Party, who became its first chairman, was Herr Friedrich Thielen, a Bremen businessman who had been the leading light of the Bremen Branch of the Deutsche Partei and Herr von Thadden became vice-chairman under him. During World War II von Thadden was a Panzer officer and just before he joined the N.P.D. he was head of the Deutsche Reich Partei many members of which followed him when he left it. He is now the real leader of the N.P.D. and having once been the editor of a paper has quite a flair for publicity. He has always denied that he was a Nazi although there is some evidence that he was a member for a few months in 1939, when he was only 18 years old. It is true that his step-brother, who later became President of the Protestant Church Assembly, was put in prison by the Nazis for belonging to the Confessional Church in which the well known member of the German resistance movement Dietrick Bonhoeffer was a minister, and his sister Elizabeth was executed by them in 1944 for "defeatism". In spite of this, however, he is on record as having said that under Hitler "there was order again in the army", which proves that he did not regard the Third Reich with disfavour.

The N.P.D. was skilfully managed even from the very early days and its leaders took great care not to put up candidates in any constituencies in which they thought they would make a poor showing, otherwise they would almost certainly have contested Berlin in the spring of 1967. Furthermore, everything has been done to play down the fact that a very large proportion of its members are unrepentant and nostalgic Nazis, "Out of twenty-four members of the Party's executive committee", von Thadden has said, "only six discharged an official function in the service of the National Socialist Party. It is felt that this percentage is not unduly high, particularly if one stops to consider that in 1945 no fewer than twelve million Germans were members of the N.S.D.A.P. or one of its affiliations, that is every fifth German."

The main tenets of the N.P.D. are as follows: looser ties with the West and objection to "domination" by the U.S.A. and Great Britain, which it describes as "white slavery"; the withdrawal of allied troops, and a federal-type Europe on the lines of de Gaulle's idea of a continent of Fatherlands (*Vaterland* in Germany, however, has an ominous ring); the end of restitution to Israel which is regarded as "blackmail"; an end to the war-crimes trials which only serve to perpetuate the legend of Germany's guilt in respect of World War II; finally, severe restrictions on foreign investors, especially those in the U.S.A. who are alleged to be "taking over German industry".

The Party also maintains that it is the only real "national opposition" and regards the three main political parties in the Federal Republic today as the stooges of Germany's former enemies. On the emotional side the N.P.D. manifesto calls for the "elimination of public immorality" and an end to the "decomposing influences of a decadent world". What is most needed are a revival of the old German conception of *Volk und Reich* and pride in their *Vaterland.* First and foremost, however, is the insistence on the reunification of Germany, the reclamation of the Eastern territories, including those beyond the Oder-Neisse line and the Sudetenland.

There is no open incitement to racial hatred nor is there any display of Nazi emblems although the posters advertising their meetings are printed in the same style as their Nazi forbears, the only difference being that in the circle the initials N.P.D. appear in place of the swastika. This is obviously done as a concession to the younger members of the Party, many of who have stated that they do not want to belong to a successor to the Nazi Party and would leave the N.P.D. if they thought that it was.

Nevertheless the anti-Jewish feeling in the N.P.D. is only faintly concealed, and the remark of its leader, already mentioned in another chapter, is proof that it is there only just below the surface. "We have no Jewish problem in the Federal Republic today", von Thadden said, in answer to a question put to him during an interview for the B.B.C., "for there are only 30,000 of them left and they are mostly old and quiet."

As was stated in a "Background Report" issued by the American Jewish Committee of the Institute of Human Relations in New York, that the official Party newspaper, *Deutsche Nachrichten* (D.N.) has accused the former Chancellor Adenauer of "selling out" Germany on the occasion of his trip to Israel in 1966. When Eugen Gerstenmaier addressed a Jewish conference in August of the same year, the second largest right-radical newspaper in West Germany suggested that it was yet another example of "Jewish blackmail". It also lambasted the noted historian, Galo Mann, as one who "does not speak for the German people" because of his pro-Jewish remarks at the same meeting. The *D.N.* has also revived old Nazi themes alleging a partnership between "World Judaism" (i.e. organized Jewry) and Bolshevism seeking world domination. It has also blamed "anti-Fascist Jews" for provoking the U.S.A.'s entry into World War II in order to justify the German destruction of European Jewry.

There has, so far, been no direct reference to the "Protocols of Zion" but it is obviously, having regard to the above, not very far distant. In the same connection, however, von Thadden referred to "the problem of Israel" where, through "diplomatic blackmail" the Jews were "continually demanding more and never stopped moaning about the past". The deduction to be made from all this by the general public in West Germany is that the N.P.D. definitely and openly accuses Israel and World Jewry of being the cause of Germany's difficulties. Nor was this all. von Thadden's self-satisfied remark about the non-existence of a Jewish problem in West Germany today is a reminder that had it not been for Hitler's "Final Solution" there would still be one.

The present composition of the N.P.D. is what might be expected from the broad appeal of its programme. At least 37 per cent of its members are between the ages of 45 and 59 who belong to a generation which was more influenced by the twelve years of the Third Reich than any other. When Hitler came to power they were between the ages of 11 and 25. The young ones were either members of the Hitler Jugend or the Bundesmadchen, and the others joined the Waffen S.S. At the time of Germany's defeat they were between 22 and 37. It is small wonder that they have a nostalgic memory of their

Führer. About 28 per cent of the Party's membership are refugees from East Germany. They want to return to their lost homelands and do not think the other three political parties in the Federal Republic are likely to bring about the reunification of Germany however much they may be giving lip service to it. These refugees want reunification to be in the forefront of their country's foreign policy. About 16 per cent of the members are under 20 years of age. They have no Nazi links and nearly all of them cannot understand how their parents apparently revered the Führer. There are, however, many things in the N.P.D.'s Manifesto which appeal to them and, of course the Party's leaders, in order to attract young people to its ranks, vehemently deny that they are neo-Nazis.

In framing its policy both Thielen and von Thadden have been extremely astute, for they have gone as far to the right as they could without incurring any risk of being banned under the terms of the present Federal Constitution. All this probably accounts for the Party's successes at the *Land* elections since November 1966, but they have also been helped, without any doubt, by the Cabinet crisis which led to the new coalition between the Christian Democrats and the Socialists under the leadership of a former Nazi, a crisis which revived the suspicion of the value of democratic government which has existed in Germany for the last fifty years.

There have been many Nazi-type political parties in West Germany since the end of World War II but none of them have been so well organized or received so much financial support. If there were to be a decline of prosperity in the Federal Republic it is not beyond the bounds of possibility that the N.P.D. would get considerable financial support from the leaders of German industry in the same way as Hitler did during the years immediately prior to his invasion of Poland in 1939. A country's big industrialists will always jump on the band waggon once they realize there is no alternative.

Another factor that may during the next few years make the N.P.D. a real force on the political scene is the very existence of this new and unexpected coalition. Few observers outside Germany itself can have foreseen that two politicians with such different political backgrounds as Kiesinger and Willy Brandt could have come together, yet this is exactly what has happened.

Will this liaison last? Time alone will tell, but even if it does the present government may well have to take certain unpopular economic steps which could possibly lead those who will be most affected by such measures to join up with the only Party in their country which promises a return to the "good old days" of the Third Reich. There are still many people who refuse even to consider the possibility of the Germans reverting to extreme nationalism in spite of her past history but the following warning which was issued by the American Jewish Committee of the Institute of Human Relations on November 21st 1966 can hardly be said to have no justification.

> The American Jewish Committee, mindful of the unhappy past in Germany, expresses its alarm at the returns of Sunday's elections for seats in the Bavarian State Parliament. The show of strength by the ultra-right National Democratic Party was the latest in a long series of events clearly indicating that *vestiges** of the Nazi era remain. Two weeks ago in a similar Parliamentary election in the State of Hesse, the Party gained its first state-wide representation, a sharp sign of the increasing spread of a neo-Nazi virus. Less than a year ago a report from the Bonn Government's own Interior Ministry showed official concern, both generally at the rising tide of radical right activity and specifically at the growth of the National Democratic Party, which it labelled neo-Nazi. An American Jewish Committee mission that spent time in Germany investigating aspects of this disturbing report and meeting with German educators and officials, expressed its anxieties both during its visit and on its return. The mission predicted that "an economic reversal or a sharp political conflict" could unleash latent anti-democratic forces.
>
> Sunday's results, which show the rising strength of the National Democratic Party confirms the worst fears of our mission.
>
> The American Jewish Committee hopes that the German leaders will intensify efforts to expand political education throughout all sectors of Society. We also urge the Bonn Government to redouble its efforts to maintain a vigilant alert in which the growth of the National Democratic Party and all the other extreme rightist elements are carefully observed, using the schools, the churches, the mass media and the courts as a grand coalition to counteract these growing signs of Nazi revival.

Others who have special knowledge of German political history,

*The italics are mine.

including Herr Fritz Allemann* have issued similar warnings and stressed the danger of ignoring them. Referring to the N.P.D.'s successes in Hesse and Bavaria he pointed out that for the first time in twelve years, an extreme nationalist movement had found considerable public support in an election in the Federal Republic, which might be disregarded were it not for what had happened in the past. Only five years before von Hindenberg appointed Adolf Hitler to be Chancellor of the Third Reich his Brown Shirts and other followers had been regarded by the majority of Germans as nothing more than a lunatic fringe. It remained lunatic in its thinking and its policy, although the word lunatic may seem somewhat of a euphemism, but it did not remain a fringe for long.

The N.P.D. successes were all the more remarkable having regard to the fact that so many other extreme right wing parties which had been formed since the foundation of the Federal Republic when they contested constituencies at a number of elections found themselves unable to obtain the necessary qualifying five per cent vote. In order to determine whether these election successes were merely a flash in the pan Herr Allemann says that it is necessary to go back to the days when the Federal Republic was in its infancy and Alfred Loritz,† who was known throughout Germany as the blond Hitler, founded a party in south-east Germany called the Wirtshaftliche Aufbauvereinigung (W.A.V.). Loritz was indeed a complex creature for he had been a member of the German Resistance Movement but hundreds of enthusiastic Nazis were attracted to him because when addressing political speeches he raved and ranted like their beloved Führer.

Both the W.A.V. and another Party, the Deutsche Reichs Partei (D.R.P.) were represented in the first Bundestag but neither of them were purely neo-Nazi. "This label", Herr Allemann wrote in an article which appeared in the Wiener Library Bulletin, "it is true, was freely applied and fitted many of their leaders and their followers only too well; many neo-Nazis were, however, nothing more novel than thinly disguised old Nazis. On the other hand, it included also a certain number

*Herr Allemann, who is the German correspondent of the Swiss *Die Weltwoche* has also written a book entitled *Bonn ist nicht Weimar.*

†See page 45.

of old-school conservatives, in the case of the W.A.V. and in that of the D.R.P., many lower middle-class and farming supporters of a rather 'poujadist' hue. Actually, the votes these parties received were mainly 'protest votes', coming to a large extent from particularly depressed areas and from refugees not yet fully integrated into the social fabric of their new environment."

This is, of course, one good reason for apprehending that the N.P.D. may receive increased support from the electors in the Federal Republic in the event of a serious slump. Those who prefer not to see the warning light from Hesse, Bavaria and Schleswig Holstein and see fit to play down the N.P.D.'s electoral successes support their optimism by giving the example of the sudden demise of the Sozialistische Reichs Partei (S.R.P.) only two years after it had been extremely successful at elections in Niedersachen and Bremen. During the Allied occupation in 1951 the S.R.P. obtained 11 per cent of the vote in Niedersachsen and a few months later in Bremen. In 1952, however, the Party was banned.

There is, however, no reason to think that the leader of the D.R.P., Dr. Fritz Dorls was not so astute. As Herr Allemann pointed out in the article referred to above, Dorls joined the Nazi Party as early as 1928. "Highly intelligent, an outstanding gifted organizer as well as a ruthless demagogue he embodied neo-Nazism in its purest form. His Party, tightly organized in accordance with the *Führerprinzip*, served by a S.S. type gang of uniformed rowdies called the Reichfront, was as clear-cut a fascist organization as has ever sprung up in post-war Germany."

It is unlikely that the N.P.D. will come right out into the open until they have become so popular and are in receipt of such support from the electorate that it would be virtually impossible to order their disbandment. Meanwhile there is much in their programme of policy which appeals to the many Germans who were disappointed with Dr. Erhard and mistrust the coalition of the C.D.U. and the S.D.P., and revives memories of Hitler's early days without having the real taint of Nazism. The plaintive cry that "barbed wire fences, death strips and the wall are cutting the nation in two" reminds one of the German diplomat who told a member of the Swiss Government in 1918 that if the Germans lost the war "they would organize sympathy," and the complaint that "alien and remote powers keep the nations of Europe in thrall and for their own political benefit prolong the division of Germany and of Europe" recalls to many Germans the partial occupation of Germany under the Versailles Treaty which they described as an "intolerable servitude". And what is the slogan "Germany first and then Europe" supposed to do except to cause the older Germans to remember the once popular Nazi song, "Germany today, and tomorrow the world". The significance of the fact that all these quotations from the N.P.D.'s Manifesto revive such memories should not be disregarded. There are many similarities between the N.P.D. Manifesto and the Twenty-five Point Nazi programme policy which was first published early in 1920 less than two years after Germany's first defeat.

These were published in *Die Tat*, a left-wing paper, on November 19th 1966 in the following form:

TERRITORIAL DEMANDS

"We demand space and soil for the maintenance of our people (*volk*) and settlement of our surplus population."
—N.S.D.A.P. Programme.

"Germany is entitled to the territories in which the German people has had its roots for centuries."—N.P.D. Manifesto.

GREATER GERMANY SELF-DETERMINATION

"We demand the union of all Germans in a Greater Germany State in accordance with the right of all peoples to self-determination."
—N.S.D.A.P. Programme.

"We demand the straining of every effort to awaken the German nation's will to self-determination."
—N.P.D. Manifesto.

AUTHORITARIAN RULE

"We demand the creation of a strong central authority in the State; the unconditional control by the political central parliament of the whole State and its organizations . . . we actively combat the demoralizing parliamentary administration whereby posts go by Party favour."
—N.S.D.A.P. Programme.

"Germany needs a State and social order which create a common purpose between the natural authority of a genuine democracy and the citizen's freedom to make personal decisions which give *to each his own* in social justice."
—N.P.D. Manifesto.

FAIR PLAY FOR THE "LITTLE MAN"

"We demand that large stores be immediately communalized and rented cheaply to small tradespeople; that for all public supplies whether national, *Land* or local, preference shall be given to small traders."
—N.S.D.A.P. Programme.

"The N.P.D. demands restriction of the big-scale, anti-social and ruinous competition arising from unrestricted development of large stores, mail-order and discount companies, etc., to the independent, healthy retail trade."—
N.P.D. Economic Resolution.

STATE REGULATION

"We demand relentless measures shall be taken against any who work to the detriment of the public weal . . . we demand the formation of committees representative of the various professions and estates to ensure the laws promulgated by the central authorities be carried out in the component states."
—N.S.D.A.P. Programme.

"The trade-union and employer's associations exist as social partners to ensure the essential balance and interests and industrial peace. This is where their task lies, not in the usurpation of political privileges. It is the economy and its organs that serve the State and nation (*Volk*) not the other way round."—N.P.D. Manifesto.

AGAINST "DECADENT ART"

"We demand that legal action be taken against any tendency in art or literature having a disruptive effect upon the life of of our people (*Volk*) and that any organizations which offend against the foregoing requirements shall be dissolved."
—N.S.D.A.P. Programme.

"The Reich Government will undertake a thorough moral cleansing of the National (*Volk*) body. The entire educational structure, theatre, film, literature, press—all will become a means to this end, they must all serve for the preservation of the eternal values in our nation land (*Volkstum*)."—Declaration of the National Socialist Government, March 23rd 1933.

"Instead of insisting on true art and real culture the managers of culture set-up as a substitute a public market of modernistic alleged avantgardismus. The responsible authorities of the state Lander and districts bear responsibility for fast advancing moral decay . . . they allow one of the oldest culture nations (*Kulturvolk*) of Europe to be delivered over to corruption and moral decay."—N.P.D. Cultural Political Resolution.

FOR "GUIDED ART"

"It is not the intention of the National Socialist State to create a culture from above . . . the task of the State is to combat harmful influences in art and promote valuable ones . . . to pursue a policy of German culture to bring the creative artists in all fields together to one united will-outlook under the leadership of the Reich."
—Preamble to the Reich Culture Chamber Law.

"In place of the parochial culture level of the *Lander*, we demand a Federal Ministry of Education, Science and Research. No one intends to deprive snobs and idlers of their 'artistic' freedom . . . we do not demand their suppression . . . But we do declare opposition to the dictatorship of charlatans and degenerates who destroy all standards and take away from beneath the feet of our people (*Volk*) the very ground on which it has grown-up."—N.P.D. Cultural-political Resolution.

UNITED EUROPE

"It is clear that our opponents will in no circumstances permit our continent to find a common basis for its affairs even in its most elementary questions of living. We know that our country can only live and prosper in a healthy Europe."
—J. Goebbels: "The Visions of a New Europe".

"Alien powers hold the nations (*Volker*) of Europe in tutelage and maintain the division of both Germany and Europe in order to achieve their own political aims . . . in place of domination by foreign Great Powers the free will of Europe's peoples must once more prevail . . ."—Foreword to N.P.D. Manifesto.

GLORY TO THE MILITARY PAST

"The Wehrmacht is the army-bearer for the German people (*Volk*). It protects the German Reich and Fatherland, the people united in National Socialism and its living space (*lebensraum*) the roots of its strength lie in a past rich with fame in Germanic nationhood, German soil and German labour."—Duties of the German Soldier (1939).

"The courageous conduct of German soldiers throughout the ages must be the model for the Bundeswehr. The service of arms is the service of honour . . . while the fathers are publicly stigmatised as criminals with impunity, the sons cannot be good soldiers."
—N.P.D. Manifesto.

It is not suggested, because of the above similarities that the N.P.D. is a replica of the N.S.D.A.P., for it is not. Nevertheless, in order to attract support it is making use of most of the same political and emotional factors which brought Hitler to power in 1933 although some of them are presented differently. Furthermore, the political events which immediately preceded the formation of the present coalition government have been most helpful, as *The Guardian* pointed out on November 24th 1966. Commenting on the recent successes obtained by the N.P.D. in the Bavarian *Land* elections the paper observed "The N.P.D. leaders affect at least a veneer of respectability, but in one sense they are more dangerous than their more moronic predecessors. For they are the focus of a dissatisfaction which has grown up after the 'German economic miracle'; after West German democracy has proved itself, after the Federal Republic has been accepted into the comity of Western Nations."

The Editor of the *New York Times*, Mr. Sulzberger, has called it a "frightening dwarf" but, in his opinion, it is the Germans who should be the most frightened, and the folly of the Christian Democrats in selecting a former Nazi as their Party leader has only served to increase the apprehension. Mr. Sulzberger is quite right, and it is for the Germans to stop the growth of neo-Nazism and remove the reasons for its rise. All Germany's present allies can do is to keep a watchful eye open. It might also be helpful if Western politicians were to talk less about the reunification of Germany and, in any event, insist on the Oder-Neisse Line.

On October 31st 1967 when the extreme right-wing Nationalist Democrats (N.P.D.) obtained 8.8 per cent of the poll in the Bremen provincial election its success was rightly described in many of the leading British national newspapers as evidence that the neo-Nazis were on the move again, despite the fact that the Party still continues to disclaim any connection with the Nazis of the Third Reich. They do this for the most obvious reasons, one of which may well be that the Party leaders realize that to admit any such connection might alarm the Bonn Government to such an extent that it would either alter the electoral law or bann the N.P.D. even though the present Chancellor, Dr. Kiesinger, has made it abundantly clear that he is not in favour of such a course.

Another and much more dangerous fact emerged, however, as a result of the Party's success in Bremen, namely that many younger people are now joining the N.P.D. than was the case a year ago. Whereas in 1966 the average age of its members was 50, it is now only a few decimal points over 40. Even the leader of Herr Strauss's party, the C.S.U.*, described the Bremen results as an "alarm signal", and he reminded them of what happened in the early 'thirties and what that cost Germany during the ensuing twelve years. Furthermore, some of the speeches made just before polling day in Bremen by Adolf von Thadden were too reminiscent of the past to be ignored. His declaration that Germany should be "liberated from the powers which have occupied and divided it" had a distinct Hitlerian flavour. It was also reported in one of the London newspapers that "an independent opinion poll carried out among N.P.D. supporters showed that 36 per cent would vote again for men like Hitler, if one appeared in Germany and a further 22 per cent refused to answer the question".

Less than two months after Bremen the N.P.D. held a congress in Hanover where according to the correspondent of the *Daily Express*, who attended it, "more than two thousand neo-Nazis leaped to their feet and cheered von Thadden for a full two minutes" at the termination of the Congress, after he had told them to be Germans first and nothing other than Germans. Von Thadden was quite sure of the future of his Party. "We shall win seats at the next general election", he said, "there is not the slightest doubt about that". "But", he went on to say, "our immediate worry is not the election but the future of the younger generation and the state of our Fatherland and, if we are asked what is the Fatherland, our answer is the whole of Germany, West Germany, East Germany, Pomerania, East Prussia, the Sudetenland, Polish occupied territory and our friends in Austria. Our programme is a clarion call to the whole of the German nation."

There was also, during this same speech, another reminder of traditional German foreign policy, the *Drang nach Osten*†, followed by Imperialist and Nazi governments alike, which produced the Neutrality Pact of Tauroggen and the Berlin-

*C.S.U. are the initials used to denote the C.D.U. in Bavaria.
†The "drag to the East".

Moscow Pact mentioned in another chapter. Although the N.P.D. would fight against communism in Germany itself, it was essential to have "a pragmatic policy of mutual interest with Russia", von Thadden told his audience, for the Russians were first and foremost interested in patriotism and peace. To spread communism throughout Europe was only of secondary importance to her. The old enmity between the former Entente Cordiale and Germany was then, once again, brought out into the open. "France opposes British entry into the Common Market", he said, "and instead of arguing with France, Lord Chalfont threatens Germany with reprisals, the withdrawal of the Rhine Army, recognition of two German States and stepping out of Berlin. So Germany must be punished because of French policy. Although we want a united Europe we will not have it by blackmail".*

When preparing this rousing oration von Thadden must have looked through the press cuttings of the other Adolf's speeches for he made this statement which is almost identical to something which Hitler said as far back as 1922. "Our movement", Hitler said, "is not sustained by money or lust for gold but only by our love of the people". Von Thadden's version was as follows: "We demand a new order, a new norm of worker on whose summit stand men and women for whom Germany has a higher value than the wallet."

He considers that the present coalition of Kiesinger and Brandt is weak and not sufficiently German because they are allowing themselves to be brainwashed by the Americans and the British, and he gave a pledge that one of the main planks in the Party's programme is to end Germany's alliance with the U.S.A. The wild enthusiasm which marked the finale of the N.P.D. Congress in Hanover brings back to many Germans only too vividly the rabble-rousing speeches of the Führer. That these same Germans, bearing in mind the disasters which he brought upon them, are still bewitched by such performances is ominous particularly having regard to the fact that von Thadden is not a man of the people, but a Prussian aristocrat and is certainly not the new Hitler from whom 36 per cent of the members of the N.P.D. say they would vote for should the

*This was a reference to the remarks made by Lord Chalfont at a press conference after a meeting of the 'Six' in October 1967.

occasion arise. What obviously attracts them is what has attracted previous generations of Germans—extreme nationalism. The programme which von Thadden summarized as follows: down with buying foreign arms; down with paying for foreign troops stationed in Germany; down with compensation to the Jews; down with giving foreign aid; down with helping N.A.T.O. allies with money. Also the cry with which the Führer ended so many of his speeches and which von Thadden echoed in Hanover: "*Ein Volk, ein Nation, ein Vaterland*".*

Whether the younger members of the N.P.D. are attracted by the same things as the older members it is difficult to judge. But even if they are not at the present moment it is not safe to presume that they will not be in the future. The Germans have always liked being shouted at, for they have a reverence for authority. They even have a word for it—*obrigkeit.*

It is more likely, however, that they are now joining the N.P.D. in large numbers for a different reason; because they are not impressed by the strange coalition between the Christian Democrats and the Socialist Democrats. Those of them who are more conservative are suspicious of Willy Brandt in the same way as many Social Democrats cannot understand why he threw in his lot and that of his Party with a Chancellor who was formerly a member of the Nazi Party. After all it was Herr Strauss, the present Minister of Finance and a leading figure in the C.S.U., who said of his cabinet colleague, "One thing Brandt should be asked: 'What were you doing all those twelve years outside?' We know what *we* were doing inside."

There is also much dissatisfaction with the diplomatic failure of Dr. Kiesinger under whose leadership, in the words used by the Bonn correspondent of *The Times*, "the German Government has performed the remarkable feat of displeasing Washington, London and Paris. The Americans suspect Germany of conniving increasingly with General de Gaulle and are annoyed with Bonn's reserves about signing the Nuclear Non-proliferation Treaty. On the Common Market issue Dr. Kiesinger is in a postion of exquisite embarrassment in his attempt to be the 'honest broker' who will persuade the General to accept Britain as a member of the E.E.C." This was only too obvious when the German Chancellor appeared at a press

*One people, one nation, one Fatherland.

conference in London during his official visit in the autumn of 1967. Later, at a Party meeting of the Christian Democrats at Pirmasens he made it quite clear that he was not prepared to try to coerce the French into agreeing to Britain's entry and he was reported as saying that "it would be all too easy to bang the table. Sometimes that looks impressive, but if it simply leads to one of the Six getting up and going out then I am convinced that it is better to avoid such a crisis than to induce it by a show of force".

If the coalition government in the Federal Republic were to break up what would happen then? Many Germans hope that it would be a good thing for German democracy if it did, but this is open to grave doubt and the most probable effect would be to strengthen the N.P.D. for this reason. The coalition is unlikely to pack up unless there is a serious financial crisis. At the present time* this does not appear to be imminent but it is quite clear that the economic miracle is over and cracks are appearing. Mass unemployment would bring the Bonn Government down and, within a reasonably short time, German democracy might follow it.

There are a number of other reasons for being uneasy about the ever increasing and attraction of the N.P.D. Competent observers in the Federal Republic who do not want to see the clock put back and are, therefore, keeping a watchful eye open are all agreed that the N.P.D. has already attracted a dangerous number of young people to its ranks.

The average age of the candidates put up by the N.P.D. and elected in the Bavarian Elections was a little over 47, and the average age of those elected in Hesse was considerably lower, namely 40. Now the latest claim made by the Party is that the average is less than 33, but that may be slightly exaggerated.

The views of Monsieur Spaak, formerly Prime Minister of Belgium and Secretary-General of N.A.T.O., that it cannot be doubted that the N.P.D. is a Nazi Party were expressed in an article written by him and published by the Belgian daily newspaper, *Le Soir*, shortly after the Party's striking successes in Bavaria.

> There has existed in West Germany since the war a Nazi force which until recently has not been clearly expressed because she

*January 1968.

did not dare to do so. Nevertheless a few weeks ago it was done in Hesse and more recently in Bavaria. Germany is now emerging from the shadow and silence behind which she has been taking refuge since her defeat in 1945. This is an indisputable and anguishing sign of the times. It is impossible to ignore the fact that the N.P.D. is a Nazi Party. Its leader has admitted that many of its leading members were formerly active Nazis. Its programme is not merely nationalistic but, also, violent by anti-American (alas this phenomenon exists in other European countries). It also contains expressions of racialism against the Jews, against the blacks and against foreigners in general which typified the speeches made by Hitler and his colleagues.

I watched a television programme which really upset me. I heard, and what is more I saw, N.P.D. candidates conducting their election campaigns and I found myself living once again through the horror of the pre-war years. The vehemence of their oratory, their heinous talk, the atmosphere which they created, all reminded me of the Nazis.

There is no doubt that the evil of the Brown Shirts is, once more, being brought out into the light of day by men who have neither remorse nor shame. After the war ended the Bonn Government banned the Communist Party. It would be difficult to understand it if the Bonn Government did not take suitable measure against this new menace to Germany's future for such blameworthy negligence can only result in placing a gulf of mistrust between Germany and the rest of Europe.

Nor have some of von Thadden's public utterances given any cause for complacency. A summary of two interviews which he gave respectively to a British and French journalist is set out below.

When interviewed by James Cameron in December 1966 he said:

We have become the tools of foreign machinations. We have lost our dignity. The German people (*Volk*) are in the course of losing their personality *which could be the soul of Europe.* This is most unfortunate for the moral integrity of Europe. Could anybody reasonably think that the Americans would come to the defence of Europe if it would endanger the security of her own country? Of course they would not. Therefore they must be got rid of. Europe only needs Europeans. Yes, we must keep on repeating that after more than twenty years it is time to get rid of the fallacious conception that Germany is responsible for all the evils of the war. We must stop raking up the past, the guilt of the Germans for the so-called war crimes whilst the thousands of other people who committed crimes against the Germans go scot-free. These trials are farcical. Shall we ever hear the last of this so-called guilt? Forty per cent of the Germans alive today never knew Hitler. Of course there are certain cases like Auschwitz *which are regrettable*, but must we go on living with this forever?

It is things like this which can bring about the moral destruction of a nation. It has become a case of international blackmail. The Jews, yes, there have been difficulties with the Jews.

Here von Thadden repeated his statement mentioned elsewhere in this book about there being no Jewish problem in Germany today.

However, the Israel problem has now replaced the Jewish one. This is what I call diplomatic blackmail. We have been paying and are still paying out large fortunes in compensation for what is called "restitution". They have never stopped moaning about the past and keep asking for more. Each time the Bonn Government gives in. How long will this continue? Is it not perfectly reasonable to believe that for two decades the political structure of Germany has been undermined by the theory of collective guilt? After all what is it we have done which is so bad?

When interviewed by a correspondent of *Paris Match* a few days later von Thadden said:

With regard to the frontiers on the West I have already stated that as far as we are concerned this was settled by the Treaty of Locarno which was willingly accepted by the Weimar Republic six years after the Treaty of Versailles when it was agreed to give up any claim to Alsace-Lorraine. The N.P.D. also stands by this and we will continue to do so. Therefore from the West we ask for nothing.

In the East, however, we demand what was taken from us but we want to obtain by agreement with Russia. We believe that the American armed forces should leave Germany. We feel that the American nuclear protection is useless and that the French should be able to keep the Russians at bay. There is no need to have millions of atomic bombs in order to make aggression unthinkable.

The inherent danger of the N.P.D. to the newly-weaned German democracy after the Bavarian Elections was sufficiently

A children's band plays at an N.P.D. meeting in Hanover

The N.P.D. faction of the newly elected Bavarian Landtag, during the constitutional session of 2nd December 1966

A demonstration against N.P.D. in which 2,000 young people of Munich took part realized by the Bonn Government to cause it to issue the following bulletin through its Information Office.

> The N.P.D. consists of about 21,000 members, seventeen per cent of whom, amounting to 3,500 formerly belonged to the Deutsches Reichs-Partei (D.R.P.) which is no longer in existence. Another 38,000 come from other extreme right parties. Other former members of the Hitler Party (N.S.D.A.P.) who joined it either before 1933 or after the seizure of power by the Nazis are still joining the N.P.D. in ever increasing numbers. It is estimated that former members of the extreme right wing parties who disappeared for a time and other former Hitlerites amount to more than half the number of N.P.D. members. Of the twenty members of the Party's executive committee nine were either members of the N.S.D.A.P. or of affiliated organizations before 1933 and were high functionaries of the Party. The weekly paper of the N.P.D., the *Deutsche Nachrichten*, has a circulation of 37,000 but as the number of its readers increased it was found that the circulation of another weekly, the *Deutsche Wochen Zeitung* fell from 30,000 to 25,000.
>
> The N.P.D. obtains its funds from the subscription of its members, their donations, special collections and from the sale of pamphlets and posters. The Party members are particularly generous with their donations because in 1965 the executive committee received D.M. 320,000. Although the proportion of former Hitlerites in the N.P.D. is large it would be wrong to regard it as an assembly of incorrigible Nazis.
>
> The *Allgemeine Deutsche Zeitung* in an article dealing with the Jews now in Germany rightly stated that it is both a temptation and a danger to regard the N.P.D. as an organized group of new Nazis. If one makes this mistake one falls short of the truth and one would misjudge this new manifestation of German political life. There is definitely a kernel of former and unrepentant National Socialists in the Party who hold key positions.

The very fact that the Bonn Government thought it necessary to issue such a bulletin clearly shows that there was, even then, some reason for alarm. Since then the N.P.D. has made considerable progress details of which have already been given. Finally, and this should cause no surprise, the new German Chancellor, Herr Kiesinger, has also tried to minimize the danger which many Germans feel owing to the rise in popularity of the N.P.D.

On December 18th 1966 he was interviewed on American

Television and denied the existence of a "serious" danger of the resurgence of "nationalism" in the Federal Republic. According to him the N.P.D. is a "complex phenomenon" and it is very difficult to know what it wants and whether it will survive. Herr Kiesinger believes that a very large majority support the Democratic parties.

This was undoubtedly true at the last General Election which took place while the N.P.D. was still in its infancy. In September 1969, however, the situation may well be very different. That the Party will survive is no longer open to doubt. It is quite clear from its manifesto and the public speeches of its leader what the Party wants and Herr Kiesinger knows this perfectly well.

The Chancellor went on to say that the conditions which existed at the time of the coming of Hitler had disappeared and that there was no chance of a return to the past. He firmly believed that the German people "in the light of their experiences" would *never* back a nationalist movement.

Having regard to the above it becomes necessary to ask what are the basic causes of the N.P.D.'s attraction for an increasing number of the electors in West Germany. They are best described by the word 'crisis' which has become one of the Party's slogans and for which it lays all the blame upon the present party system. There is not just one crisis but several.

(1) *Reunification:*
The inability of any German Government because it is "powerless" to solve the major problem of West Germany, namely the question of reunification.

(2) *The crisis of authority:*
This according to the Party leader has arisen because of the resignations of "liberal Ministers" and the inability of former Chancellor Erhard to find a satisfactory solution.

(3) The economic crisis with which Germany has now for many months been threatened.

(4) *The European crisis:*
Many Germans above all the younger generations are becoming disillusioned because they sincerely believed that a united Europe would, by now, have become a reality.

(5) *The Army crisis:*
Discontent among the more senior officers in the Army who

do not like the present subservient state of the force and wish for more power. This was recently brought out into the open by the resignation of a number of high ranking officers. A great deal of support for the N.P.D. can be expected from the armed forces.

(6) *The International crisis:*
Cracks are beginning to appear in the allied bulwark in Germany due to the American intervention in Vietnam, the difficulties in which Great Britain finds herself and the withdrawal of France from N.A.T.O.

These crises, whether they are real or imaginary or even only exaggerated, provide most favourable ground for a neo-Nazi breakthrough because they all concern matters which are so close to the hearts of many Germans.

During the last party conference held by the N.P.D. its leader Adolf von Thadden, now familiarly known as Adolf II, prophesied that after the parliamentary elections in September 1969 his party would have not less than fifty seats in the Federal Parliament.

The recent *Land* elections in Baden-Wurtemberg, which were held on April 28th 1968, have clearly shown that his optimism was not unjustified. The percentage of votes obtained by the N.P.D. was only fractionally below 10 per cent, and was 2 per cent more than the previous maximum percentage which the party obtained at the elections held in Bremen. Moreover, it is not without significance that this latest success has been gained in a part of Germany which was not one of the strongholds of Nazism during the Third Reich. And the considerable reduction of votes suffered in the same elections by the S.P.D. is an indication that, if the electors in the Federal German Republic are dissatisfied with the present government of their country, they are more likely to turn to the Right than to the Left.

It may be argued that the N.P.D. can be of little danger to the new German democracy if it only holds fifty seats in the Bundestag, but to say this is to ignore what happened in Germany during the last few years of the Weimar Republic just before Hitler came to power, and the indisputable fact that, however vehemently the leaders of the N.P.D. may deny it, it is a party of the extreme Right, whose manifesto is in many respects identical to the Nazi Party programme.

It may also be argued that the main reason for the defeat suffered by the S.P.D. in Baden-Wurtemberg is the dissatisfaction of many of its former supporters with their party's decision to form a coalition with a party under Chancellor Kiesinger. There is, undoubtedly, some truth in this, but unfortunately there appears to be little, if any, likelihood that this coalition will be broken up. On the contrary, these two parties have decided to close their ranks even further, which bodes ill for the future. If the S.P.D. were now to leave the coalition and become once again the main opposition party, German democracy would get its second wind, and this is what is clearly needed. The violent Left extremists led by Rudi Dutschke would lose many of their supporters, the middle classes would be less afraid of the future, and the N.P.D. might well lose some of its present supporters.

But even then the general picture of West German politics would not be too rosy. It should not be forgotten that as each month goes by there is increasing evidence that more young people are turning with hope and expectation to the new Adolf. In the early days of the N.P.D. most of its supporters consisted of those who still have some nostalgia for the Third Reich. A recent survey conducted by experts in the Bundeswehr has revealed that, by September 1969, when the elections will be held for the Federal Parliament, one German soldier in every two will vote for the party which puts German nationalism, with a capital N, in the forefront of its programme.

The recent demonstrations of the extreme Left have contributed to this. What von Thadden, in effect, told the voters during the election campaign in Baden-Wurtemberg, was this: Here we have a government which is incapable of stopping an uprising and which trembles before the students. If you want the re-establishment of law and order vote N.P.D., because we know how to deal with these hot-heads.

Chancellor Kiesinger himself said that the violence of the students had frightened the electors, and that this was the reason for the N.P.D.'s latest successes. The fact that these same electors threw themselves into the arms of von Thadden is a reminder that the Germans during the early thirties, faced with the scarecrow of Bolshevism, fell into the arms of Hitler, and it could happen again.

In some countries, but particularly in Great Britain and the United States of America, the attitude of many people to the political events of the past two years in the Federal German Republic has been, like ostriches, to bury their heads in the sand. The result of the elections in Baden-Wurtemberg, however, seems to have had some impact. The Bonn correspondent of the *Daily Mail* has stated that the success of the N.P.D. was due to the fact that it based its electoral campaign on "the exclusive pursuit of the strictly national interests of Germany by arguing that she should withdraw from N.A.T.O., send home the foreign troops at present on her soil, and negotiate with Russia from a position of strength for the return of the territories which she has lost to the East". It is small wonder that this policy has borne so much fruit, as it is one that must be close to the heart of every German, for it is embedded in their past history.

During the recent elections Chancellor Kiesinger said that the whole world had its eyes fixed on the electors of Baden-Wurtemberg. A member of his government said, off the record, to the Bonn correspondent of one of the leading Paris newspapers that, should the N.P.D. obtain 7 per cent of the votes, it would be extremely serious in a *Land* like Baden-Wurtemberg, which was traditionally democratic and not inclined to extremism, but if it were to obtain 10 per cent that would be a veritable sign of alarm.

The warning note has already sounded. It is to be hoped that it will not fall upon deaf ears.

There can be no doubt that the N.P.D. will still be well in the picture in September 1969 and it is for the reasons given above that the signs of a revival of Nazism, call it neo-Nazism, nationalism or what you will, should not be ignored, and it is the Germans themselves who, more than anyone else, should take note of them.

CHAPTER SEVEN

The Trustees of German Democracy

The reason why I have dedicated this book to the Youth of Germany must be obvious, for they are indeed the trustees of German democracy. It is, however, proposed in this chapter to enlarge upon it. The future of Germany does not lie in the hands of those who were politically active during the Third Reich nor those who have been administering and governing the country from the early days of the Allied Occupation up to the present time. Whether the new democracy, which is still in its adolescent stage, is to succeed or to go the way of the Weimar Republic must depend upon political decisions which will be made by comparatively young people of both sexes who were just old enough to have served, even if only for a short time in the Hitler Youth (Hitler Jugend) and by an even younger generation born after all these things happened.

This is, of course, fully realized by the present rulers of the Federal Republic and by the leaders of the various parties and organizations on the Nazi fringe which have come into existence since the war. It is because of this realization that the latest arrival on the political scene, the N.P.D., is trying so hard to attract the young people to its fold by playing down its nostalgia for the past, by concealing as far as it can its strong links with the Nazi past and by using the shortcomings of the Erhard administration, to persuade the younger generation that under a democratic government Germany will never recover its former power and glory.

Since the war ended a very large number of new youth organizations have been formed but the danger of these has, at times, been exaggerated because so many of them have not really had any political affiliations of any kind whatsoever. At the same time it is equally dangerous to underestimate their possibilities. It is for this reason that Kurt Tauber in his book on German nationalism since 1945* regrets that so many journalists have been tricked into playing the "number game on the unsound assumption that 'numbers don't lie' and that they can tell an accurate story". Even as reliable a newspaper as *The Times* has estimated the number of young people in post-war Germany who are members of nationalistic youth groups, to be as high as 200,000 which was the same figure as that given in 1959 in a left-wing journal called the *Socialist Youth Correspondence.* In the same way, but for a different reason, the Federal Government has stated that the number is not more than 3,000.

Apart from the obvious political reasons for exaggerating or underestimating the number they are, according to Kurt Tauber three other factors primarily responsible. The first and most important is the difficulty of determining exactly what constitutes a nationalist, neo-Nazi or militarist youth organization. The second is the complexity of the organization of these groups many of which from time to time often temporarily merging, later break up into splinter groups. They retain the same leaders and frequently the same or similar names, which makes it almost impossible not to count the same organization twice. This results in adding to the total number. The third reason is the fact that since 1960 the number of organizations has been constantly diminishing.

The chief cause of these discrepancies, however, is that misleading estimates are deliberately given for political reasons, two examples of which have already been given above. Nevertheless, some estimates which have been given are beyond dispute, one of which resulted from a confidential opinion poll of young Germans between the ages of 18 and 24. This showed that 56 per cent wanted Germany to return to a régime of a one-party state. The deduction to be drawn from this, however, is not so frightening as it might appear at first sight for the poll took place in 1952, only seven years after the end of the war, which means that all those who had been interviewed probably served at one time or another in the Hitler Jugend. These same people are now between the ages of 33 and 39 which is the main reason why it is, to a great extent, upon the next generation that the future of Germany depends.

***Beyond the Eagle and Swastika.*

The generation which immediately preceded them, most of whom had served in the Hitler Jugend or the Bundes Madchen* during the most formative years of their lives, regarded the Führer almost as a deity. Even other youth organizations which were not affiliated to the Hitler Youth Movement felt the same way about him as the following article written by a youth who was a member of the Evangelical Young Men's Association of Germany clearly shows.

> I shall give obedience to the German State [he wrote], This is for me not in the least difficult, as long as a man like Adolf Hitler leads the Third Reich. I revere this unique German man from the bottom of my heart . . . it was not the parliament of desiccated liberals which made him its puppet, rather the Germanic *Thing* of the people's fellowship has proclaimed him the new German Duke. There is hardly another people which is capable of offering its leader—for the sake of his genius as a statesman—the kind of unconditional obedience which the German people are capable of offering. I am happy to be one of those Germans.

This quotation is a striking example of the effect upon the youth of Germany of the heady wine of Nazi propaganda. No wonder that there was instilled into the minds of myriads of young Germans absolute submission to the Führer's will. No wonder that the principle of "*Befehl ist Befehl*"† became the overriding commandment of the Nazi faith.

Even members of the famous Scholl family, of which two, Hans and Sophie, were later murdered on Hitler's orders for being members of the German Resistance,‡ had been influenced earlier on by the spirit of the Hitler youth. This is what Sophie's sister, Inge, wrote:

> We heard much talk of the Fatherland and comradeship, the people's community and love of homeland. We were impressed and we listened with enthusiasm when we heard it discussed in the school or on the street. . . . But there was also something else that attracted us with mysterious power and pulled us along. That was the mass marching columns of youths with their unfurled flags, their eyes straight ahead and with drum beats and songs.

*This was the equivalent of the Hitler Jugend but was composed exclusively of girls.

†An order is an order.

‡See *Conscience in Revolt*, by Annedore Leber.

Was this comradeship not something overwhelming? Thus it was no wonder that all of us joined the Hitler Jugend. We were part of it body and soul . . . Was it not splendid to have something that we young people could share, that connected us with young people whom otherwise one would, perhaps, never have come close to? . . . We heard that we were to live for a great idea. We were taken seriously and this gave us a curious kind of uplift.

This is quite understandable but one is left in doubt as to whether the "uplift" would have been so great and so satisfying had some of these young people known at the outset what was going to be expected of them later.

The Hitler Jugend was to become the forcing house for future S.S. men, and a body of adolescent fanatics under its leader, Baldur von Shirach, about whom the Nuremberg tribunal said this in their judgment:

After the Nazis had come to power von Shirach, using both physical violence and official pressure, either drove out of existence or took over all youth groups which competed with the Hitler Jugend. He educated German youth in the spirit of National Socialism, and subjected them to an intensive programme of Nazi propaganda. He also established the Hitler Jugend as a source of replacement for the Nazi Party formations and entered into an agreement with Himmler under which members of the Hitler Jugend who came up to Nazi standards would be considered as the primary source of replacements for the S.S·

The propaganda which was pumped into these youths was full of the iniquity of the Versailles Treaty, the need for *Lebensraum*, the theory of the Master Race, the Führer principle; and they were imbued with what the Nuremberg tribunal described as "the noble destiny of German youth to die for Hitler". Von Shirach "planted into the young generation the great tradition of death for a holy cause, knowing that with their blood they would lead the way towards the freedom of their dreams.*

The training of the Hitler Jugend was organized on military lines with uniforms and quasi-military ranks, the object of which was, in the words of von Shirach's deputy, to ensure "that a

*These words are from a speech by Admiral Raeder on German Hero's Day, 1939. The freedom referred to was stated in another part of the speech to be the "freedom to re-arm".

gun feels just as natural in the hands of a German boy as a pen". During the war thousands of former Hitler Youth members, then in the Waffen S.S., committed war crimes throughout the occupied territories, such as the massacres at Oradour-sur-Glane and Le Paradis. Many thousands more blood-thirsty ruffians were waiting impatiently to take the places of those who fell.

Russian children were even used as live targets for the musketry training of the Hitler Jugend. A Frenchwoman named Ida Vasso, who was manageress of a hostel for aged Frenchmen in Lvov during the German occupation, said that she had seen this happen and her statement was fully investigated and confirmed. The report of a commission which investigated these allegations stated that in Lvov the Germans "spared neither men, women, nor children. The adults were simply killed on the spot and the children given to the Hitler Youth for target practice".

It is not surprising, therefore, that when the Third Reich, which these youngsters had been told would last for a thousand years, fell in ruins they became bitterly disillusioned. Their revered leader, who was to have been the saviour of Germany, had gone with it, and their belief in absolute and unquestioning obedience also disappeared. This is how it was described by a youth who had joined the Hitler Jugend in the early days of the war:

> When the collapse came all was empty inside me. Was everything we had considered right now suddenly become wrong? At that thought more broke down within me than merely faith in the Movement. Who could still be trusted? Did not the things we had been taught have the ring of candour and truth about them? And now we were told that all those words for the sake of which we would have gone through fire and water were lies and deception. I stood before an abyss. After that kind of experience can any man be trusted? My faith in the whole of mankind began to waver. This inner fissure can heal only slowly with the passage of time.

Former members of the Hitler Jugend who felt like this young man are unlikely to change their minds, but his reaction was not shared by all the others. Some of them took a very different view although they were in a minority. Nothing that had happened had shaken their confidence or their faith in Hitler and what they thought he stood for. They did not blame their Führer but the "traitors" who had tried to get rid of him. It is they who are the nucleus of the anti-democratic forces which exist in the Federal Republic and might well be the foundation upon which a dangerous revival of Nazism could be rebuilt.

Nevertheless, the general impression one got of the young people one met, especially those at the universities, when visiting Germany between 1960 and 1963, gave encouragement for the future. Perhaps one of the most heartening demonstrations of a possible change of mind has been the annual pilgrimages made by thousands of students to the mass graves of those who met their deaths in the concentration camp at Belsen, which prompted the President of the Social Democrats to state that "among the young people there is an increasing readiness not only to leave behind the awful past but also to create a more humane and free order". It would be unwise, however, to become too optimistic on this account and anyone who has paid a visit to the site of this former concentration camp during the past few years would be unlikely to do so. It is only a short afternoon's motor ride from Hamburg and hundreds of people make the trip every Sunday in the same way as in London they go to Hampstead Heath or in Paris to the Bois de Boulogne. In the camp there is nothing to remind people of the atrocities which were committed there, as there is at Auschwitz, Dachau and Ravensbrück. The only inscriptions to be found on the mass graves merely indicate that "Here lie 3,000 dead", and the national monuments only state that they have been erected in memory of "those who died for their country".

On the other hand the report which was published in the official journal of the Circle of Christian Democratic Students stating that "at least 70,000 German youths are now active in a federation of radical right-wing organizations" is equally inaccurate and misleading. The editor of *Der Spiegel* has summed-up the attitude of the younger generation of Germans better than anyone else. "Youth here", he has said, "does not despise moral values but, like the youth of other nations, it knows little of them." This is one of the reasons why so many young Germans have been saying that so far as the government of their country is concerned they wish to contract out, "*ohne mich*" (without me) they are inclined to say. Fortunately there is reason to believe that this negative approach to politics is no longer so universal.

An article written in the well known newspaper *Die Welt* in May 1959 entitled "What do students think about the Jews" deals with the way in which the young people's minds have been influenced, albeit unconsciously, by what they have gathered from their parents about Nazi anti-Semitism. After describing the frequent "pilgrimages" to Belsen the article continues as follows:

> This number, growing year after year, seems to confirm the oft-stated optimistic thesis that while anti-Semitic feelings are still prevalent among members of the older generation, today's youth, however, confronts the Jewish problem without prejudice and without preconceived ideas. But is the situation really that good?
>
> We must take it for granted that the virus of Nazi propaganda is rampant. "Everything that *Der Sturmer*, Rosenberg and Hitler said about the Jews lives on." This pessimistic statement was made recently on the subject "Anti-Semitism at school", during a teachers' conference held in Hamburg. The speaker did not invent it. As principal of a high school in a large city in the Rhein-Main area he had questioned 150 seniors on the history of the Jews in Germany and on problems which, according to their opinions, should still be solved in connection with the Jewish question.
>
> The result of this survey was disheartening. Suspicion, cynicism and "smart-alec" attitudes characterized the replies, factual knowledge was vague and slogans from the Nazi period were often repeated. Proved facts refuting Nazi doctrines were doubted. Many of the statements contained in the answers given by those who were interviewed could not have been the result of the students own experiences and it was clearly their parents prejudices which had prompted the replies.

But perhaps the most emphatic evidence on the appalling lack of knowledge on the part of the younger people in Germany about the Hitler period was disclosed in a report on this subject which was shown on German television in May 1959 and reported in the *New York Times*.

> A television crew took the camera and microphone into scores of West German classrooms . . . They found that nine out of every ten students between 15 and 17 years of age knew nothing about Hitler or believed that on the whole he had done more good than

harm . . . The students were asked, "What do you know about Hitler?" It was found that one in ten gave what was considered an intelligent reply namely, that Nazism was a "concoction of the anti-Semitic Nationalist and Socialist beliefs latent in the German people at that time". But for every one such reply the Television encountered nine others which set German educators' hair on end. "Hitler revived Germany. He cured unemployment and built the autobahns" was one of the most general. One student said, "After the war people said that everything he did was bad and they pointed to ruin and chaos everywhere. But now people come again and say it was not so bad after all". Another said that he was able to judge Hitler positively because "we are free again, or at least half of us are" and a third said that the only thing she knew was that he "ruled from 1933 to 1945".

There is no doubt that before the unfortunate anti-Jewish outbreaks which occurred just before Christmas 1959 the history books in West German schools hardly gave any coverage at all to the events which took place between 1933 and 1945.* Every effort was made to omit more than a casual mention of the horrors committed by the S.S. both within Germany itself or in the territories occupied by the Germans. Early in 1960, however, after these incidents had caused considerable alarm outside Germany, and were deplored by the resident President and Chancellor of the Federal Republic as sullying the name of Germany, steps were taken to improve the instruction of German youth concerning what the Federal Minister of the Interior called "the guilt and disaster of the Third Reich". The Minister, in a speech made to the Bundestag, gave a list of publications issued by the Office for Political Education which appeared quite formidable but the fact remains that they were read by very few people and not used in any schools. Nevertheless, he admitted, that it was obvious from what had recently happened that a great deal still needed to be done, and he promised that immediate steps would be taken to ensure that it was.

Another point that he made, and anyone who has visited Germany and gone thoroughly into this subject would agree, that there has been this difficulty and that it still exists, was that the school teachers are not prepared to take all the blame for the inadequacy of the instruction regarding the events which

*See Chapter III.

took place during the Hitler régime because, as they said, it was a responsibility which they shared with the educational authorities, the Churches and, above all, with the parents and politicians. Some schools and teachers had, without doubt, neglected their duties for various reasons, such as convenience, lack of courage or understanding, secret sympathy for National Socialism, or questionable objectivity. Many teachers also found that they were under pressure from parents who did not want their children to learn the truth about Hitler for the obvious reason that when the subject had been taught in school it frequently resulted in their children, when they came home, asking their parents most embarrassing questions. In addition to this there was the desire of the older generation to forget and suppress not only the chapter of the Third Reich but the entire history of Germany. As one German writer has put it, "Since the whole of the past seems to be besmirched the Germans decided not to have a past". This resistance on the part of the parents resulted, as one history teacher complained, in the facts taught during history lessons being challenged and "pulled to pieces" at home by the parents.

It was a German historian, Hans Rothfels, who said that this desire to forget has never been a way to healthy recovery. "We cannot run away from contemporary history", he wrote, "if we wish to understand ourselves and take up a position in relation to what is to come . . . there must be a methodical search for truth."

A commission of educational experts, theologians and historians was, therefore, appointed to advise the Government as to "what focal point in political education should best be concentrated upon having regard to our recent history". Two of these subjects were "the imparting of correct information regarding the persecution of the Jews, and the totalitarian abuse of power under the Third Reich".

The following principles were then laid down by a conference of the Education Ministers of the various *Lander:*

(1) That in the examination for the teaching profession all candidates must satisfy the examiners that they are familiar with the basic rights of the citizen, have a general knowledge of German history since the beginning of the twentieth century and know the main facts which led to the

destruction of constitutional government under the Nazis.

(2) That school libraries must contain the basic works on recent history.

(3) That historical and political facts should be described and discussed objectively in schools.

These principles, however, were of no practical use because they did nothing to ensure that the real history of the Third Reich was brought to the attention of school children. The mere fact that the teachers knew the true facts was no guarantee that they would pass them on, the "basic works on recent history" were completely inadequate, and the discussion could be entirely one-sided depending on the attitude of the teacher himself.

Nevertheless, during the next two or three years a great improvement did take place, and in many schools the senior pupils began to learn more about the past and could no longer pretend that all they knew about Hitler was that he had cured unemployment and built the autobahns. Moreover, in some of the schools arrangements were made for the history of the Hitler period to be taught by young teachers who could not be asked the embarrassing question which was so frequently put to the older ones, "What were you doing when all this was going on?" Even then, however, the trouble really began when the children went home and started discussing with their parents what they had been taught in school.

But it was not until the war crime trials conducted by the Germans themselves were in full swing that many of these young people began to learn the whole truth and nothing but the truth, and they were deeply shocked, to such an extent that the nation tended to become divided into age groups. Many of their elders were as annoyed as their children were shocked, because, for the most obvious reasons, they objected strongly to the Nazi crimes being brought out into the open so long after the war had ended.

This was not, however, the only reason for their objections. When the war crime trials were being carried out by the Nuremberg Tribunal and by the Allied Military Courts in the various zones of occupation the Germans protested that it was wrong that the vanquished should be brought to trial by the victors, but when the trials began to be conducted by the

Germans themselves another excuse had to be invented. In most of these trials the accused have been charged with murder and for this reason, owing to the fact that there is a statutory limitation of twenty years for such charges, the period has, quite recently, had to be extended. This, in the eyes of many Germans was considered to be unfair, but they have also raised another objection. These crimes were only committed, they say, because their country was engaged in war and wars create special circumstances. These men were not murderers in the real sense of the word and it is unfair that they should still be tried for having committed these crimes twenty seven years afterwards.

Nevertheless, one member of the team of German lawyers which is concerned in bringing these criminals to trial has said that to confuse these trials with trials for war crimes is madness. "The result has been that the German people combine these two categories in their minds. It provides an easy way out. The Russians, they say, were killed because they were helping the partisans, and the Jews would not have been killed either if it had not been for the war. But this is not true. The Nazis killed out of principle: the *Untermenschen*—the sub-humans—were there to be used as slave labour until they died of starvation or were killed. The Nazis said so. Its murderers we are after. It's our duty to prosecute murderers".

Anyone who is familiar with Hitler's *Mein Kampf* or the programme of the N.S.D.A.P. must be aware of the fact that what the German prosecutor stated about the Nazis admitting that they "killed out of principle" is supported by unimpeachable evidence. Point Four of this programme stated that, "only a member of the race can be a citizen. A member of the race can only be one who is of German blood, without consideration of creed. Consequently no Jew can be a member of the race". This masterpiece of German logic was preached throughout the length and breadth of Germany from the moment of Hitler's accession to power. The Jews were to be regarded as foreigners and they had no rights of German citizenship. They were expendable and that is why registration, segregation, humiliation, degradation, deportation, exploitation and extermination were to be the milestones on the road of suffering along which these unfortunate Jews were to make their last journey.

(*left*) Fritz Thielen, founder of the N.P.D. and its first chairman.
(*right*) Dr Fritz Dorls, leader of the D.R.P.

Chancellor Konrad Adenauer shakes hands with former Defence Minister, Franz-Josef Strauss, during a party held by the Christian Social Union in October 1963

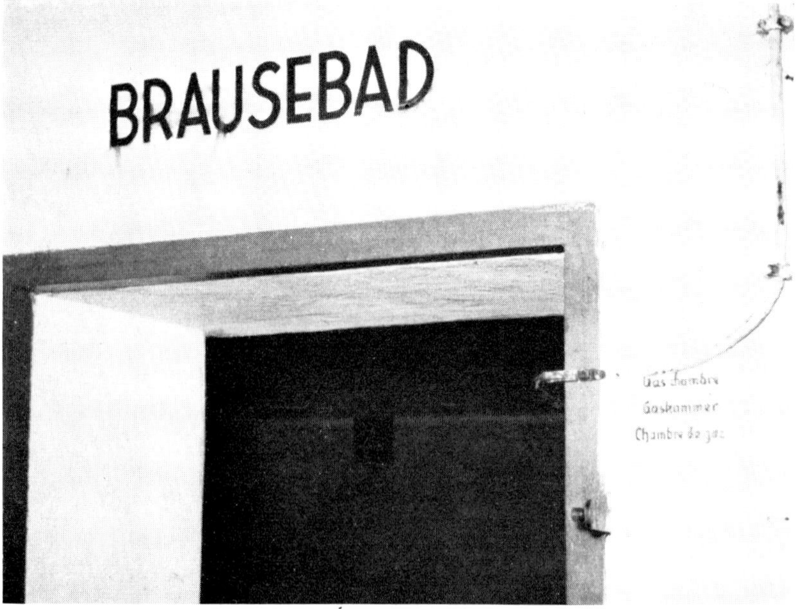

The door to the gas chamber at Dachau, showing the German word for 'shower-bath' painted above it

N.P.D. leaders at the graves of war criminals executed by the Allies at Landsberg prison

Finally, in the official journal of the S.S., which was called *Das Schwarze Korps*,* it was stated that "just as the Jewish Question will be solved in Germany only when the last Jew is gone: so the rest of Europe must realize that the German peace which awaits it must be peace without Jews".

This doctrine was accepted without question by all of Hitler's underlings and, fearful that he might be accused of not carrying it out with sufficient speed, Hans Frank when Governor-General of Poland, made this apologetic note in his diary: "I could not, of course, eliminate all lice nor all Jews in only a year, but in the course of time this end will be attained."

Is it any wonder that many young people who have only learned about all this within the last few years say, as one young German has, "how can we even mention these things to our parents. How can we let them think that we connect them even remotely with these terrible events. It would dirty our family and our love . . . I have had very difficult moments with my parents. I have asked them many questions. Normally we get on extremely well, but they cannot answer about the past—its taboo."

Nevertheless, there are some young people who just cannot believe half they hear and think the trials should come to an end. "In any event", some of them say, "the people who are being tried were just soldiers and they were only obeying orders." To the majority of Germans that excused everything. It may be, however, that this attitude is due to the fact that because the Nazi crimes are now part of history they cannot in any way be related to the present. An illustration of this was given in an article which appeared in the weekly colour supplement of the *Daily Telegraph*†. One of the State Prosecutors working on Nazi criminal trials visited a youth club in Hamburg and told them about a man living there who only a few weeks earlier had come to him of his own free will and confessed that he had volunteered for service in the famous S.S. Division 1005. "He told me he shot children," the prosecutor said, "but he didn't even know how many, though he thought it was about 114. He had made them kneel down near a pit, then stood behind one after the other and shot them in the neck. He knew

*The Black Corps—named after their black uniforms.

†"Generation without a Past", by Gitta Sereny. May 5th 1967.

of eighteen other S.S. men in Hamburg who had been in the same Division. There was dead silence among all the young people until one of them, a girl, suddenly said, "Did you hear that? Eighteen men like that now living in Hamburg volunteered to shoot children! It gives me goose pimples." Gitta Sereny was present during the conversation and, she wrote, "I was certain that this had been the first time she—possibly all of them—had connected this horror-tale of the past with today, their city and their homes."

It is, therefore, not surprising that some of the school teachers find the task of teaching the history of the Third Reich almost impossible. As one of them has said, "How can I talk about these things when at one desk sits a child whose father was in the dock at Nuremberg and at another a child whose father was in a concentration camp."

This kind of difficulty, of course, is likely to diminish as time goes on for every year more young teachers enter the profession and the main problem, which is one of generation, will gradually cease to exist. At the present time, almost half the teachers were in their twenties during the war and most of them were probably enthusiastic followers of the Führer and are more inclined to remember the good times they had and forget the horrors which many of them accepted automatically without thinking. These things were done in the course of duty and were inherent in their being good loyal Germans. It is, therefore, not surprising that they are inclined to skate over events like the "Final Solution" of the Jewish Question, slave labour, and the massacre of the civilian population in occupied Europe, of which, when they look back, they are, perhaps, more than a little ashamed.

Already there have been some signs of improvement and, provided it continues, there is reason to hope that each year more young people will emerge from their schools and universities with a fuller realization of the errors of the past and better equipped to take an active part in ensuring that they will not be repeated. There is, however, one danger, namely, the long-standing reverence of the German for authority, but among the young it is, fortunately, not so prevalent. The younger generation in most countries today are more inclined to kick over the traces than were their elders whom they regard as "squares".

Many parents condemn this tendency and there is something to be said for this attitude. In Germany, however, it can do nothing but good, for between 1933 and 1945 their elders cannot be said to have given them a good example.

Whether this optimism is justified may depend to some extent on the effect which service in the armed forces has upon the young men who have to serve a term of conscription in them. When the Bundeswehr was first formed on the rearmament of Western Germany service in it was not at all popular.* and the army itself was as different as chalk from cheese compared with that which existed under Kaiser Wilhelm and Hitler. This change was not to the liking of many of the older officers and *feldwebel* who preferred the old system of unquestioning obedience, and to some extent their will has prevailed. What the effect of this will be still remains to be seen.

Finally it is necessary to consider what the attitude of the youth of Germany to the N.P.D. will be. Nearly two years ago the *average* age of its members was 50, now it has fallen to 40 which means that many of them were still in their late teens when the war ended. Why are more young people joining the Party? Is it because of its extreme Nationalism or have these new members merely been attracted by its recent success in the provincial election in Bremen where 8.8 per cent of the votes were obtained?

The leader of the N.P.D. is himself only 45 years old and this, in itself, must attract the young. He is also confident that at the next election his Party will be returned to the Bundestag with at least 40 seats and will then be in a position to "influence national policy-making", and what he has now in mind can be seen by reading the Party's Manifesto. This prophecy, and it is by no means a wild one, must also attract younger members to the N.P.D. for there are few young people today who, to use their own expression, do not want to be "with it".

One of them who joined the N.P.D. immediately after he had finished his military service, said that he was not attracted to it by "those fat old men who sit around with beer mugs in their hands boasting of the women they had in Paris". They made him sick. But, he went on, "you have to understand, I can get a chance in their party. Go round, do things, speak on

*See Chapter II.

the platform, sit on committees, organize. Where else would I get the chance?"

The young, or many of them, are disillusioned with the present, and are looking to a new future. It is to be hoped that they will not build it on old foundations.

The Summing Up

In the foregoing chapters of this book an attempt has been made to set out briefly and objectively the underlying current of extreme nationalism which has persisted in West Germany ever since her defeat and unconditional surrender in 1945. There are outward signs of it from time to time, especially the outburst of anti-Semitism in December 1959; the constant attempts to play down, or forget the best and even to pretend that it never existed; the glorification of Hitler by many writers and in the memoirs of generals and others; and the rise of a comparatively new political party, the N.P.D., which in spite of the subtle denials of its leading figures can fairly be described as neo-Nazi, and which has a definite attraction for the average patriotic German, as well as for those who still look back over the years when Hitler was in power with nostalgia, and, which is more alarming, is now beginning to attract many young people who have become somewhat doubtful about the efficacy of the new democracy.

For reasons which have already been given there was cause to doubt, even during the first two or three years of the Allied Occupation, whether the leopard would change his spots.

Some years later when the decision was made by the three Western Allies to re-arm the Germans because of the fear of Russia's intentions, those who were old enough to remember it could not keep recalling the fact that it was because of the German fear of Bolshevism that the Weimar Republic came to an understanding with the German Officer Corps, and this inevitably resulted in the revival of militarism and eventually led to World War II.

During the years dealt with in Chapter II, after the abandonment of Allied controls, many events took place which did nothing to dispel the understandable pessimism of those who while they prayed for the success of democracy in West Germany could not ignore the lessons of past German history.

The Naumann Plot, the Zind case, the formation of the Deutsche Soldaten Bund and its newspaper, the Deutsche Soldaten Zeitung edited by men who had once served in the Propaganda Ministry under Goebbels, and the demonstrations staged in many parts of Germany by the Stahlhelm under former General Remer with the help of Kesselring, Ramckes and Rudel, all pointed in one direction.

But these were not the only straws in the wind. There was the scandal caused by the refusal of Dr. Adenauer to dismiss one of his chief political advisers, Dr. Globke, who had been head of the Office for Jewish Affairs in the Ministry of the Interior under Hitler, in which the Nuremberg Laws were drafted.

Another disturbing feature is the large number of judges and members of the civil service, all of them former active Nazis who still remain in important posts and about whom nothing concrete has been done despite persistent criticism in certain German newspapers.

The long battle to obtain compensation for the victims of Nazism, particularly those who happened to be stateless and had no one to stand up for them, was convincing evidence, which no responsible person could fail to notice, that the Germans were completely unrepentant about the past. Indeed the views of the Bonn government itself were made crystal clear by the Minister of Justice who said that "no compensation should be paid to victims of the Nazis until justice had been done to the whole German people."

Until the sudden and unexpected successes gained by the N.P.D. in some of the *Land* elections, beginning with Hesse in November 1966, there was still cause for some optimism and there seemed to be little or no reason why the Bonn Republic should meet the same fate as its foredoomed predecessor. The West German press is still independent and many newspapers have criticised the Federal government for its attitude to such problems as compensation for the victims of Nazi persecution, the trial of war criminals and pensions granted to former Nazi officials.

On my first visit to West Germany nine years after I left it in 1951 the situation appeared to be more hopeful. Having been able to talk to all kinds of people young and old, official and non-official throughout the whole of the country I came away with a feeling of optimism. There seemed little reason to think that the new democracy would meet the same fate as the Weimar Republic and there appeared to be very little danger that it would. The future, however, rests in the hands of the younger generation, those who are today not much more than thirty years old. The older Germans were not then greatly interested in politics. So much in their world has changed that all most of them seemed to want was to live and die in peace, prosperity and, above all, oblivion. However, the resurgence of what the Germans call right-wing radical thinking, now embodied in the N.P.D., has altered this attitude to some extent and they now feel that they have a *point d'appui*.

In 1960 the majority of the middle-aged group felt uncomfortable for so many of them were compromised by the past. They did not like their children coming back from school, where by that time, a little more was being taught about Hitler than was done previously, and asking the famous question, "What did you do in the War Daddy?" Now that they have a political party whose leader has stated that the Germans have "nothing to be ashamed of with the exception of incidents like Auschwitz, which are regrettable," they feel re-habilitated. The great danger is that they are still young enough to take a leading part in Germany's future.

In the early days of its re-formation, as has already been described, the army also appeared to have no resemblance to the Wehrmacht or the Reichs wehr, but it was a small incident which brought the changes home to me more than anything else. I was in Göttingen watching some new recruits being given tank driving instruction. On my left was the Brigade Commander and standing nearby were the squadron commander and the regimental serjeant-major. In the turret of a tank which was just about to be driven off was a young soldier. Suddenly he took a comb out of his pocket and combed back his rather long hair. No one said a word. Nothing could have been more eloquent; that was enough for me.

Since the rise in the N.P.D.'s fortunes, however, the situation has changed. The older officers in the armed forces, and particularly in the Army, now realize that they have a political force behind them; a party which quite openly glorifies the former military might of Germany. It is not surprising, therefore, that the N.P.D. will obtain ever increasing support from the Germany Army.

Another aspect of current thought in Germany is the refusal of so many Germans to admit the errors of the past, and their tendency to pretend that the crimes committed by the Nazis are pure invention or at the least have been grossly exaggerated. I had an insight into this when I visited the site of the former concentration camp at Dachau, near Munich, some years ago. I had of course seen it before, very shortly after the end of the war. I was accompanied on my second visit, which took place in 1961, by a former German general, who had been introduced to me by the Americans at an army depot on the very site of the concentration camp itself. Unaware that there was very little about Dachau that I did not already know he tried to convince me that the gas chamber and the crematorium ovens had been built by German prisoners on the orders of the American occupation forces after the War, as anti-German propaganda. "The so-called gas chamber," the general said, "was really a shower bath," and he pointed out the word "*Brausebad*" painted over the door. "That," he said, "proves what I say. Had it been a gas chamber the Americans would have put up a notice to that effect. They put up notices everywhere." The General, whose name was, unfortunately for him, Unrein was obviously very stupid, and clearly thought that I was even more so. He surely ought to have realized, and I am sure he did, that had the "so-called gas chamber" been built on American orders as anti-German propaganda, they would have painted the word "gas chamber" over the door and not "shower bath".

I hastened to inform him, what I was quite sure he already knew, that the word "*Brausebad*" was painted over the door so that the wretched victims should think they were, in fact, going to have a shower bath. But I told him that it really was a gas chamber and I showed him the pipes through which the gas entered the chamber.

He still maintained that it was not and never had been a gas chamber. "Besides," he said, "it would have been impossible to burn six million Jews in half a dozen ovens unless it had begun in 1906."

He had worked it all out and it was useless for me to tell him, as I tried to do, that at least four million of them had been gassed in the concentration camps of Auschwitz and Birkenau, and the extermination camps of Treblinka, Chelmno and Sobidor, all of which were in Poland; that at one time, when Rudolf Hoess was commandant, about 10,000 were gassed in Auschwitz every day; and that in many other concentration camps in Germany, such as Belsen, Buchenwald and Dachau itself, hundreds of thousands were either shot dead or died of starvation. He would not believe a word of it, and for the second time he said, "These ovens were built by German prisoners after the war."

"Yes," said the driver of my car, who was walking round the camp with us, "Everybody in Munich knows that."

"You see, Lord Russell," the General said, "I have never met this man before, but he thinks the same as I do."

It was no use, and I said no more, but these two men are not, unfortunately, alone in their opinions. There are many others who keep up this deception and it appears to convince them that these horrible things never did happen, but, as one student said to me with callous realism, when we were discussing the difficulty and embarrassment which he experienced when he talked with his parents about the Third Reich, "One of these days they will all be dead."

The coming of the N.P.D., however, has somewhat changed the position. The flame of ultra-nationalism has been rekindled, and it is not beyond the bounds of possibility that many of them will still live to see a return of much which they regret disappeared in 1945.

After the end of the Allied Occupation and the continuation of the war crime trials by the Germans themselves, what many young Germans heard for the first time startled them. Since the N.P.D. came into existence, however, the views of many of these young people, as I found out for myself when I last visited Germany in May 1967, have begun to change. This is probably due to the insistence of von Thadden that there should be an end to these "one-sided trials for redeeming the past, while on the other hand millions of war crimes committed against German men, women and children go unpunished." The Party demands "equal justice and a final closing of the account by a general amnesty." The party also regards those who tried to get rid of Hitler in July 1944 as traitors, and objects to the glorification of high treason and "the assertion that Germany alone is responsible for the ills of the world".

But perhaps the greatest danger of all is the knotty problem of reunification, for even those politicians in West Germany who realize that it is unlikely to come about in the foreseeable future will never admit it, as to do so would be political dynamite and they would be certain of losing their seats at the next election. I have asked many of the members of the three parties who are represented in the Bundestag whether they do not think it dangerous to keep up this pretence, because when it is generally realized that it can only be attained upon Russian terms (which would involve Germany leaving N.A.T.O.) the ensuing disillusionment would be equally dangerous. One of these politicians whom I questioned agreed that it might, but went on to say, "When I say so in public, as I have done once or twice, I get into trouble with my party and am told, 'You may think it but you must not say it'."

The leaders of the N.P.D. do not find the question of reunification embarrassing, nor does the other difficult problem of the Oder-Neisse line worry them, for they are both in the forefront of the Party's policy as set out in the Manifesto. In fact it is because the N.P.D. blames the other parties for not having done anything to bring reunification about that it has received much of its support in the last two years. The N.P.D. deplores the division of Germany, the barbed wire, walls and watch towers that tear the people (*Volk*) in two. This division, according to the Manifesto, remains because the policies pursued hitherto have proved useless. Furthermore, the Party also blames the progressive integration of West Germany into the Atlantic power bloc for perpetuating this division. Alien powers are accused of assuming guardianship of the peoples of Europe for their own political aims, and, so long as the Germans submissively accept this division and Bonn does nothing to end it, the "national tragedy will continue". "Right stands before might and once we are resolved to take responsibility for own destiny and the future of the generation to come, our will to unity will be stronger than any might."

It is probably this aspect of the N.P.D.'s policy which attracts more support than anything else. The $64,000 question of reunification appeals to the innate nationalism of all Germans. There cannot be a united pacified Europe without a re-united *independent* Germany. Therefore Germany for the Germans—Europe for the Europeans. It is the same old theme of Imperialist Germany and Nazi Germany, and there are very few Germans who do not fall for it.

Nevertheless, all is not yet lost. One sign that democracy and parliamentary government are gradually obtaining some roots among the people is the existence of the Federal Constitutional Court (*Bundesverfassungsgericht*), which was set up in 1951 and sits in Karlsruhe. It is something quite new and had no parallel in the Imperial or Weimar days. One of its functions is to look into "constitutional complaints" brought by individuals against the State. In the "other Germany" any idea of challenging the authorities would never have been tolerated, but today more and more ordinary people are beginning to do this and enjoy doing so. It is a right which they would be most unwilling to have taken from them, and while there is still a representative parliamentary government in existence this will not happen. The real value of it, however, is proved by the fact that it is not very popular with the Ministry of Justice. One of the ministers frankly admitted to me that many decisions of this Court pleased neither his Ministry nor the Government, but I told him that this proved how essential it was. As one of the Court's judges said, "The fact that the Court exists is a reminder to all government authorities and officials that their action may be subject to examination and in that way may dispose them to act only within the Constitution."

So far the N.P.D. has not openly attacked this priceless constitutional safeguard, but it is quite obvious that many facets of the Party's policy could not be carried out unless this Court was abolished or its powers drastically curtailed. Nevertheless, the Court is, and has been, almost since its formation, besieged by litigants, and this cannot but be a good thing and an indication that more people are beginning to realize, for the first time, that they have civil rights, and that it is they who are important and not the State. Is it not possible, however, that the majority of Germans have not got so used to this new German political conception that they would miss it very much should it suddenly disappear. It is too early to give the answer to this but it is also too early to be certain either way.

Until recently there were few signs of a dangerous revival of nationalism in Germany. One reads from time to time in the press of new youth organizations run on the lines of the notorious *Hitler-Jugend.* One such organization was the Bund Nationaler Studenten but its total strength in 1960 was only .63 per cent of the total number of university students in the whole of the Federal Republic, and in most of the universities they were regarded with contempt and derision as a lunatic fringe. But today many students who would never join anything so reminiscent of the Nazi days as the Bunder Nationaler Studenten are quite prepared to join, and are in fact joining in considerable numbers a respectable political party like the N.P.D., which is still heavily camouflaged and has much to offer.

Furthermore, unless the new coalition does much better than is generally anticipated, and a serious economic depression should take place within the next two or three years, the N.P.D. could be a real danger to democracy. Once something of that kind were to happen and there was a swing from the licensed parties to the right wing radicals, the N.P.D. would come right out into the open and get rid of its camouflage—the iceberg would no longer be two thirds under the water, and democracy, which has always been a sickly plant in Germany, would quickly wither and die.

Unfortunately many people in Germany are trying to play the N.P.D.'s election successes down, and are pointing out what is undoubtedly true, namely that the percentage of votes is quite small. It is still more unfortunate, however, that many of those who are now shrugging their shoulders and asking what there is to worry about are the very people who only six years ago were watching closely for the slightest crack to appear in the foundations of the new German democracy. I discovered this during another visit to Germany in the spring of last year, when I attended the consecration of a Memorial Synagogue at the former concentration camp at Dachau and the burial of the ashes of an unknown political prisoner on the site where a memorial is shortly to be erected in memory of those who died in the camp as the result of torture, ill-treatment or starvation. The Comite International de Dachau, which consists of former inmates of the camp, decided to hold this ceremony before the completion of the memorial monument in order to call attention to what the committee considered the new dangerous political trend in the Federal Republic, and a declaration was read out by the President of the Committee.* The declaration expressed the Committee's misgivings and uneasiness in view of the "revival in West Germany of the old *spirit* of Nazism". It called attention to the votes obtained and the seats won by the N.P.D. in the elections in Hesse, Bavaria and Schleswig-Holstein, and the Party's programme which in so many respects closely resembled that of the Nazis. These were of such significance, in the view of the Committee, that it appealed to the Government of the Federal Republic and to the good sense, reason and responsibility of the German people to ensure that there should never be a repetition of the terrible crimes committed in the concentration camps during the Nazi reign of terror.

During this visit I spoke to many ordinary Germans, including some whose views I know to be pro-democratic and violently anti-Nazi, and I was alarmed by their complacency, for it reminded me of the attitude of so many Germans to Hitler in the years immediately preceding World War II.

The N.P.D., these people said, was of no importance, and the seats won by them in these elections did not indicate *any* danger of a Nazi revival. They were nothing more than a flash in the pan, and were only brought about by the ineffectiveness of Chancellor Erhard's government during the previous eighteen months.

Unfortunately there are no indications that the present leaders of West Germany are the least bit frightened, although there are some exceptions. One of these was the Minister of Agriculture in the Bavarian Parliament, Doctor Alois Hundhammer, and perhaps it is more than a coincidence that he was himself a prisoner in Dachau. He was in no doubt about the possible dangers, and insisted that a careful watch should be kept on the activities of von Thadden and his Party.

*General Guerisse, known in the Resistance as Pat O'Leary.

It is perhaps easier to understand, although it is equally disturbing, why so many people in countries which were not occupied by the Nazis have already forgotten what happened and appear to think that it could never happen again. It is all the more essential, therefore, that the Germans themselves should pay attention to the warning for it would be folly to ignore it.

APPENDIX I

Manifesto of the National Democratic Party of Germany (N.P.D.)

GERMANY HAS now been divided for two decades. Barbed wire fences, death strips, watchtowers and the wall are cutting the nation into two. The policies so far pursued have failed to overcome the division of Germany which the victors of the Second World War imposed.

The progressive incorporation of West Germany into the Atlantic power block and the complete control exercised by the Soviet Dictatorship over East Germany, threaten to perpetuate Germany's division and that of Europe.

Our nation is being swallowed up by two hostile systems. While the East Germans remain deprived of their right to self-determination, many West Germans thoughtlessly forget the national peril. Alien and remote powers [*Raumfremde Machte*] keep the nations of Europe in thrall, and for their own political benefit prolong the division of Germany and of Europe.

Yet the German nation on neither side of the wall and the barbed wire fence does not want its country to become the battleground of fractricidal strife. It does not want to fight for alien interests. It wants unity, freedom and peace!

However, Germany can achieve unity in freedom only in a Europe truly independent and powerful enough to defend its own independence. As long as the German nation meekly accepts its division and the Federal Government does nothing to overcome it, the tide will not turn. However, once we are resolved to take the responsibility for our fate and the future of coming generations into our own hands, our desire for national unity will prove stronger than all opposing forces; because right shall ever prevail over might. We believe, therefore, in a German policy that is not subservient to foreign interests. Without a reunited and independent Germany there can be no unity or peace in Europe. Hence, Germany first and then Europe.

GERMANY FOR THE GERMANS—
EUROPE FOR THE EUROPEANS!

We call on all Germans eager to serve in this cause to help us. We address ourselves particularly to the young and those millions of disillusioned voters, who will no longer put up with the party establishment in Bonn and its claim to exclusive power and support from public funds. Our people have not deserved the leadership they get. It is no longer wanted!

In our national, liberal and social approach we represent the political movement of emergent German unity in European Europe.

National Democratic Party of Germany

OUR POLITICAL PRINCIPLES

I

Germany needs a constitutional and social structure which creates out of the interplay between the national authority of a true democracy and the personal freedom of the individual citizen that sense of communal dedication and social justice which will give each what he deserves (*Jedem das Seine*).* Germany needs a government concerned with the substance rather than the appearances of things.

The squandering of public money on prestige objects, empty representation, and monumental buildings must be stopped. We protest against the growing corruption in the circles which have taken over public offices. The true reward for public service is neither money nor power but the satisfaction of duty well performed and the resultant respect the civil servant enjoys.

II

The farmers, middle classes, skilled workers, and the risk-taking independent businessmen form the backbone of a healthy economy. They must be supported, encouraged, and protected from foreign interests and the unjustified depredations of big

*This much used slogan supposedly epitomising Nazidom's social approach also adorned the gateway into Buchenwald concentration camp.

business. While taking reasonable account of export requirements, our economic and commercial policies should ensure that home-based productive capacity is given the maximum opportunities for development. We oppose the growing control exerted by foreign investment and the sell-out for our basic industries to international trusts. The preservation of our own, independent raw material and power basis is of paramount importance. They alone vouchsafe to us freedom of political action.

We demand public control over prices to preserve the value of our currency, wages and savings. We demand radical tax and economic reforms and a unified federal tax and finance structure.

III

Not unrestrained materialism but rewards and recognition according to achievement, respect of private property, and the right to work must become the principles on which a just economic and social order can be based.

The claim of the German worker to secure employment takes precedence over those of foreign workers. Only additional work will increase the gross national product. Those who want to work harder ought to be encouraged. We demand, therefore, that overtime should be exempt from tax and social security deductions and that the earnings of those who work on after retirement age should be tax free.

Trade unions and employment confederations are partners in the economy and their job is to reconcile conflicting interests. This rather than the acquisition of political privileges is their proper function. The economy and its organs are meant to serve state and nation and not vice-versa.

IV

To maintain political independence Germany needs a prosperous agriculture. The necessary precondition for this is to provide the farming community with wages and rewards comparable to those offered by industry.

In order to enjoy security in our industrial society, agriculture must have a guaranteed income. This necessitates marketing arrangements for the food growing industry, which, based on free and independent trade associations, protect both the producer and the consumer.

V

At foreign bidding we pay to far away countries billions which serve neither Germany nor European interest. At the same time urgent development aid should mainly be confined to training schemes and technical assistance, and benefit German or European political objectives.

We oppose the continued payment of hidden subsidies and demand that all development aid, restitution payments and arms gifts be publicly accounted for. Plans for the renewal of our urban and rural regions and for an adequate transport system must be given priority. They must conform with current technical requirements and have due regard to our position in the centre of Europe. Only such planning at home will allow man to retain command over the machine stay of the centre of life.

VI

The preservation of public health is a pre-condition for our standing as a nation of cultural and industrial eminence. The provision of medical care for mother and child and for the working population is one of the first duties of state and society.

All citizens must receive adequate retirement pensions. Disabled ex-servicemen and prisoners-of-war whose release has been unduly delayed (*Spatheimkehrer*) are to receive special honorary grants irrespective of other social benefits.

VII

Germany needs a conscientious, open-minded and broadly-educated young generation, which can hold its own against the enslaving blandishments of communism and the levelling temptations of our vulgar mass-civilization. We demand, therefore, that German youth be given a uniform system of primary and secondary education which provides for the advancement of the gifted student irrespective of wealth or home background. The sciences are unfettered, responsible research is to be specially encouraged. Instead of the parochial "cultural independence of the *Lander*" we demand a Federal Ministry of Science, Education and Research.

A conscientious government must pay special attention to the upbringing of physically fit citizens. Hence the state ought to encourage every kind of sport in schools and clubs, materially as well as ideologically.

VIII

Our youth, with the tacit acquiescence of every responsible authority outside the home, is exposed to the machinations of the traffickers in sex and to every corrupting influence of a depraved society. But it wants and needs clean and decent models. Hence we demand an end to public licentiousness, which daily offends the honour of womanhood. Parents must once more be enabled to attend to the upbringing of their children. We demand that the family is given the place it deserves in a civilized nation. Large families are to be given special privileges by the state and society.

IX

We need opinion-forming media, free, responsible and in keeping with the traditions and aspirations of an ancient and civilized nation. We demand, therefore, the abolition of the corrupting, monopolistic hold on public opinion enjoyed by radio, film and television companies. It has become well nigh intolerable that a cynical clique should be able to denigrate and ridicule all pure social, national and moral values. The shocking increase in crime is one of the consequences of such infamy. Our women and children must no longer be allowed to provide easy sport for depraved criminals.

An independent judiciary must defend and uphold the constitution and the fundamentals of the rule of law against all comers. We demand that judges be shielded from governmental intervention and the intrusion of irresponsible mass media into matters still *sub judice*. Our judicature must not yield to pressure from foreign powers. Twenty years after the end of the war, we demand an end to our one-sided efforts to redeem the past by war crime trials, while other countries fail to punish the million-fold war crimes committed against German men, women and children. In the interest of Germany's domestic pacification we demand equality before the law and *a general amnesty.*

X

Germany, for the sake of her future, needs a historically truthful picture of her past. We reject the glorification of treason and the allegation that Germany alone is responsible for most of the world's misfortunes. Acceptance of such assertions leads to the moral self-destruction of the nation. Hence we demand an end to the lie of Germany's exclusive guilt, which serves to extort continuously thousands of millions from our people.

The German soldier's bravery throughout all periods of history must become a model to the Bundeswehr. To serve in the armed forces is an honour and a privilege. The soldier must know the values he is defending, and he must be sure that he is not, like a hireling, expected to serve alien interests. The sons cannot become good soldiers as long as the fathers are branded publicly and with impunity as criminals.

XI

Germany has a right to the lands from which, over the centuries, the nation has grown. While we do not dispute any nation's right to its ancestral home [*heimatlichen Siedlungsraum*], we are equally determined not to cede any of our own territorial rights. If such claims would appear to be negotiable, our position in international law would be seriously affected when it comes to defending our nation's most vital interests.

XII

The cowardly spirit of subservience and the admission of our collective guilt has paralysed German political activities for two decades. Only a people conscious of its own worth and national dignity will command general respect and gain the good will of other nations. Neither help nor assistance will be extended to a nation whose leadership, in an effort to be everybody's friend, neglects her own vital interests.

The domination of alien, big powers must be replaced by the free, untrammelled self-assertion of European nations. We, therefore, demand that the utmost exertions be made to awake in the German people the will of self-determination.

German policies ought to be based on the assumption that the peace of Europe and the world depends to a large extent on a central European rebirth brought about by Germany's unity and freedom. As long as the highly-charged fields of force of opposing power blocks cut through Germany and split Europe, the world will continue to teeter on the brink of war. German national policies are, therefore, in the world's deepest sense a policy of peace.

APPENDIX II

Appeasement, 1951 Style

EARLY IN 1951 there were already many demonstrations against the allied occupation particularly in Niedersachen and North-Rhine Westphalia. Leaflets were pushed under the front doors of houses occupied by the British and walls were daubed with signs calling on the occupying troops to go home. A swastika had been painted in white at the junction of a private road which led to the house in Vlotbo where I lived. This was doubtless due to the fact, which was well known, that as Deputy Judge Advocate General of the British Army of the Rhine I was responsible to the Commander-in-Chief for all the trials of German war criminals which took place in the British Zone. A few days before the incident set-out below my wife had been spat at by a German in the village where my house was situated.

On the evening of the last Saturday in March 1951 my wife and I left home at 7 p.m. to motor to the Officer's Club in Bad Oeynhausen where we intended to dine. The shortest and usual route was through the village of Vlotho on the outskirts of which we lived. The only alternative route involved a detour of at least twelve kilometres. When we reached the road leading to the main street we were unable to proceed any further, for we met a torchlight procession moving towards the centre of the village. We waited for it to pass and then followed. When we reached the main street into which the procession ahead of us began to move, we found it packed with spectators and a group of policemen stopped us. I asked in German what it was all about.

The procession, which had attracted the entire population of Vlotho and many hundreds from the surrounding villages and hamlets, was in celebration of the opening of a new bridge over the River Weser which had been performed with fitting pomp and ceremony that very afternoon.

The local inhabitants had, quite unnecessarily, blown up the old bridge a few hours after the unconditional surrender in 1945 and for that reason had been made to pay for the construction of the new one. This had touched the pockets of each one of them and they were determined to get full value for their money by staging a torchlight procession and a firework display. The reason for the excitement was explained to me by one of the policemen who told me that it was quite impossible to get though the crowd behind the procession, and that there was no alternative but to make the long detour. As this would have made us very late for our appointment I sent for the Vlotho police inspector whom I knew quite well. I explained my difficulty to him and he detailed a policeman on a motor cycle to ride beside us, placed a constable on foot in front of us and told us to proceed slowly along the main street in the direction of our destination.

All went well for a couple of minutes while we motored at walking pace through the crowd with our German escort. Then, without warning pandemonium broke loose. One of the spectators who had noticed that the car was English shouted "Englischer Sweinhund" and the crowd immediately surged round it. The German police made no attempt to stop them and quickly vanished and left us to the mercy of the hostile crowd. My wife and I were left to the wolves and we experienced a very unpleasant ten minutes before we finally got through the crowd who were in an ugly mood. Both doors of the car were pulled open but we managed to close and lock them. I was punched several times on the head and my hat was knocked off. Someone in the crowd tried to pull off my wife's pearl necklace, but failed to do more than scratch her neck. We were spat upon and attempts were made to overturn the car and set fire to it.

Fortunately I kept calm. Otherwise, had I put my foot down on the accelerator as I was sorely tempted to do, for I was afraid of what might happen to my wife, there would have been many casualties. However I kept on driving at a snail's pace until we eventually got through the crowd, and although attempts were made later to rake up evidence in order to trump up some kind of case against me the German police chief was only able to produce two Germans, one of them a policeman, who had received some bruises from their fellow countrymen during the general mêlée. I had little time to think but in the flash of a second I remembered an article written by Goebbels in the *Volkischer Beobachter* of May 29th 1944, in which the German people were incited to punish Allied airmen who had been shot down over Germany. "It is only by the use of firearms", he wrote, "that we can protect the lives of enemy pilots shot down during bombing raids, otherwise these men would be killed by the sorely tried population. Who is right here? The murderers who, after their cowardly misdeeds, expect humane treatment from their victims, or the victims themselves on the principle of 'an eye for an eye and a tooth for a tooth'? This question is not difficult to answer. It appears to us intolerable to use our soldiers and police against the German people who are only treating child murderers as they deserve." I could not but compare this attitude with the normal treatment which German aviators received in like circumstances.

When at last we were clear of the crowd I stopped to see what damage had been done to the car and was surprised to find that there was hardly a scratch. The crowd had been pressed so close to the sides of the vehicle that no one had been able to do anything. While I was doing this another policeman came up and demanded my papers. Although he was not entitled at that time to do this I took my pass out of my wallet and handed it to him saying, "There you are." His only reaction was to shout in German, "Speak German we don't talk English here."

There was never for one moment any doubt that no effort would be spared by the British High Commissioner to try and make out that it was all my fault. At that time the mood in the Control Commission for Germany was one of courtship. The word had already been passed round that we must woo Germany over on our side for the coming showdown with Russia. So that the evidence would not be all on one side, therefore, as soon as I reached Bad Oyenhausen I sent for the Provost Marshal (S.I.B.)* and made a full report, during which time he was able to note that I was as sober as a judge. My dual capacity of military judge and British peer made it essential to establish the fact that I was not as drunk as a Lord.

I was certain that as the incident took place on a Saturday night after dark someone would try to say that I was drunk,

*Special Investigations Branch.

although no one who knew me in the Army would have believed it for one moment. How right I was became evident when *The Times*, alone of all newspapers, published, under the headline "Germans reply to Lord Russell", the following: "Onlookers became angry (according to certain German statements) when children were frightened by the oncoming car and appeared to think that the driver was under the influence of alcohol."

That night I decided to prepare a full statement which I intended to hand to the Chief of Staff next morning, and when during the small hours I was besieged on the telephone by hordes of newspaper correspondents I kept strictly to the terms of that document when answering their questions. From the Army I received much sympathy and every possible assistance. There was no doubting what they thought of it all. On the Tuesday morning I read, again in *The Times*, that Colonel Stewart who held a post called Chief Public Safety Officer for North-Rhine Westphalia would travel to Vlotho that day to make a *full* investigation. I naturally thought that a *full* investigation would include me but although Colonel Stewart visited the German police in Vlotho he never came near me. I then knew that my worst fears were going to be realized and that for political reasons I was to be butchered to make a Roman holiday.

My wife and I, therefore, caught the next aeroplane to Northholt and on my arrival I went straight to see the Lord Chancellor, Lord Jowitt. He had already seen reports from the High Commissioner and had read mine as I had sent him a copy of it. I had ended my report with these words: "I regard this assault as a very serious matter. Had those living in the village of Vlotho been warned that traffic through the village could not be allowed that evening we could easily have made arrangements to start earlier and drive to Bad Oeynhausen via Exter and the autobahn. In any event as the German police allowed my car to proceed along Langestrasse and even proceeded it to clear the way, they failed totally in their duty by leaving us to the violence of the mob and making no attempt whatsoever to protect us. Had we ourselves been in the wrong, which we were clearly not, it would even then have been their duty to protect us."

Having questioned me fully on these reports the Lord

Chancellor completely exonerated me from any responsibility for the incident although he disapproved of my having given a statement to the press. This I had no option but to do. Had Lieut.-Colonel Keith Briant who had been an exceptionally able Chief Public Relations Officer at Rhine Army Headquarters still been in Germany I would have refused to say anything to the Press in the sure knowledge that he would have issued an accurate and adequate statement to the Press agencies. All I needed was for the truth to be told. Briant had, unfortunately for me, left Germany two months earlier and his successor was not so experienced.

Lord Jowitt then wrote a draft statement to be read in the House of Commons and showed it to me. This clearly stated that "it would" be unfair to blame Lord Russell for the incident". I was, therefore, astonished and enraged when I read in Hansard for April 17th after my return to Germany that these words had been altered to read, "it might be unfair". The difference between the two versions could not have been more damaging. I protested to the Lord Chancellor, who was himself extremely annoyed and he told me in confidence who had changed the vital word.

The damage done was, so far as it could be, put right by the answer to a question which Mr. Anthony Marlowe, the member for Brighton asked the Foreign Secretary on April 29th. The following is an excerpt from Hansard.

> Mr. Anthony Marlowe asked the Secretary of State for Foreign Affairs whether he would publish a summary of the evidence on which it was decided to withdraw Lord Russell of Liverpool from his appointment in Germany.
>
> Mr. Younger, (the Minister of State): As my Rt. Hon. friend stated in reply to the Hon. Member for Brighton, Mr. R. Winterbottom, on April 17th, Lord Russell is to be withdrawn from Germany because it was felt that in consequence of the publicity already given to the case he might find himself, however much he may desire to avoid it, becoming a focus of political feeling in Germany, and it was considered wise to take account of this possibility. Lord Russell is not being withdrawn because of the original traffic incident (*sic*) in regard to which the Lord Chancellor takes the view that it would be unfair to blame him. There is no evidence to publish with regard to the withdrawal of Lord Russell because the whole matter was dealt with by the

Lord Chancellor who subsequently had discussions with my Rt. Hon. friend.* I may add that the High Commissioner and Lord Russell have agreed between themselves that the incident should be regarded as closed and I would commend this conclusion to the honourable and learned member as eminently sensible.

Mr. Marlowe: Does the honourable gentleman realize that there is grave apprehension among other British officials in Germany that their task will be made much harder if they do not have behind them the backing of the British Government? Does he realize that we do not get respect and co-operation of the German people by showing weakness?

Mr. Younger: "I do not want to add to the trouble which has been caused by this incident, but I repudiate any suggestion that this is a case of the Government not standing by officials. I said in my answer that the Lord Chancellor took the view that it *would be unfair* to blame Lord Russell for the incident: it was not the incident but the publicity and the inevitable result of the publicity which had to be taken into account.

The above is an illustration from the author's personal experience of the appeasement policy which was already, a mere six years after Germany's total defeat, being adopted by the British Government and to some extent by the Government of the United States of America, the result of which time alone will show.

*This was Herbert Morrison.

APPENDIX III

German Anti-British Propaganda

A FILM called *Ohm Kruger* which is supposed to be the story of the Boer War was shown in London a few years ago as part of a programme called "As Others See Us". In it Queen Victoria is depicted as a secret drinker whose greed led Britain into war with the Boers, and Joseph Chamberlain as her evil genius. Sir Winston Churchill is cast as a brutal and callous concentration camp commandant. *The film was made by the Nazi government in* 1941 *as anti-British propaganda.*

It was not only the Nazis who invented this false propaganda about the British concentration camps. Many German newspapers in 1902 told the same story and contained cartoons depicting Joseph Chamberlain, Lord Salisbury, Lord Roberts and Lord Kitchener as bloody barbarians. A special magazine was also published in the same month, entitled "The Bloodbook of the Transvaal", which contained twenty-four drawings showing British soldiers kicking and beating Boer women and children, and Chamberlain raking their corpses into a mass grave.

The legend of the British concentration camps has been passed on from father to son in the Union of South Africa ever since 1902 and was made much of by the Nationalist Party which was very anti-British and pro-German during World War II.

When in May 1945, the horrors of Hitler's concentration camps were laid bare when they were liberated by the Allied Forces, many Germans tried to turn the tables by pretending that the concentration camp was a British invention. What are the true facts?

On March 13th 1900, after Bloemfontein, Lord Roberts issued a proclamation allowing those burghers who laid down their arms and took an oath of neutrality to return to their farms and carry on with their normal occupations. Many did so, but a large number broke their oath and started guerilla warfare under General De Wet.

This naturally led to the systematic destruction of farm-houses because they were being used as bases from which the guerrillas carried on their raids.

Refugee camps were therefore started to house the women and children from these farms who would otherwise have been left to starve or to the tender mercies of the Kaffirs who were hostile to the Boers. Very shortly after the camps were started an opportunity was given by Lord Kitchener to President Steyn to take over their occupants, but he refused to do so. The Boer leaders, in fact, approved of the camps, and De Wet himself, in his book *The Three Years War*, has recorded General Botha as saying, "One is only too thankful nowadays to know that our wives are under British protection."

It was not long before the camps became a great embarrass-ment and an administrative headache to the British because the vastness of the problem had not been realized soon enough. An appalling epidemic of typhoid broke out, and the medical services broke down. Inflexibility and red tape contributed their share to the general chaos and misery.

But it was not only in the camps that the outbreak of enteric raged. By the middle of 1900 there were 4,000 cases in the Army alone, and in those days the death rate for enteric even in the best available conditions (e.g. one of the large London hospitals) was about 20 per cent. It must also be remembered that the medical knowledge of those days cannot be compared with that of the present day; antibiotics were non-existent, and antispetic medicine generally was in a rudimentary state.

Nevertheless, notwithstanding all the above, during the worst period in the camps the percentage of inmates who died was less than 3 per cent. Furthermore all died of disease, most of the adults died of typhoid and nearly all the children of measles . . . None of the inmates was forced to work. None of them died o starvation. None of them was wilfully killed.

The inmates did little to help themselves. The insanitary habits of the Boer women contributed to the epidemics. Although there was adequate latrine accommodation in every camp, both the women and children did what they normally did on their farms, they fouled the ground all around. They were also extremely backward and ignorant and used all sorts of quack remedies, some of which might almost be called "witch's brews". The following are some examples.

(1) A child with pneumonia was varnished all over the chest and stomach.

(2) Dog's blood was given as medicine.

(3) One mother in a camp clipped the fur off a cat, roasted it and applied it to the chest of her child who was suffering from bronchitis.

(4) A black hen was split open and applied, bleeding, to the chest of a patient as a cure for inflammation of the lungs.

(5) Two children suffering from bronchitis were given sardines instead of the prescribed milk, and another was fed with goat droppings soaked in oil. Both these children died.

Having lived for years surrounded by dung, the Boer women appear to have developed a reverence for it, and it appears to have been a panacea for almost every complaint, e.g. a mother and child recovering from typhoid were given a concoction of horse's dung boiled and strained.

The camp diet was in fact better than that given in those days to peace-time soldiers. Certainly Reichsführer Himmler would not have approved. It was far too good for him, e.g. 7 lbs. flour per person per week; 3 lbs. meat per person per week. Vitamins were in those days completely unknown, however, as it was not until 1912 that Dr. Funk propounded his vitamin thesis, and it was many years after that before it became generally recognized. Nor was there any serious complaint from the Boer inmates regarding rations. As most of them said, "We know it is war time and we cannot expect much."

Life within the camps, even when conditions did not permit the issue of passes, was not altogether dull. Musical and dramatic societies, reading rooms, home industries, carpentry, games and sports were all encouraged. Concert parties visited the camps and every means of interesting the occupants was attempted. The only musical concert heard in the Nazi concentration camps was given by the "orchestra of death", as it was called, which was formed by one commandant to play as the inmates were marched away to the gas chamber.

During the whole of the time these British camps were in existence inspection by the Red Cross representatives was always allowed.

How did these lies really get started? It was natural that when things went wrong in the camps, as they frequently did during the Boer War days, they would be seized upon by the Boers and magnified for propaganda purposes. It is also natural that when the Germans were at war with the British Commonwealth and her Allies in 1914-18, they should encourage a rebellion in South Africa and whip up anti-British feeling by making use of such stories and inventing some of their own.

As a result there has grown up amongst those susceptible to such propaganda a belief that there was murder in the camps. Colonel Martin, who wrote a book on this subject* gave some examples of how these rumours gained currency.

Thus, dysentery was not dysentery, but the result of ground glass in the food, Epsom salts, much used in the camps, is supposed to have suggested this line of attack. The presence of occasional blue particles in the sugar was also said to be proof that poison was being placed in the food. In those days blue was used in the manufacture of sugar, an ultramarine or analine blue, harmless and edible, to improve the colour of the sugar. Without it, instead of the sugar being pure white, it would have been an unappetising yellow. The washing process which followed was not always successful in removing all the blue particles. The simple folk of the Veldt would not be aware of this. There was even an accusation that fish hooks were placed in the bully beef. But as this was manufactured in America it can only reflect on the mentality of those who made it and those who believed it.

This kind of propaganda was going on in South Africa to my knowledge as recently as 1956, and apparently it is still going on. Not only is it still going on, but a book was then in use in the Transvaal schools which was obviously written with the object of spreading this propaganda amongst the young. The book, which is written by a Dr. Otto, stated that the British Government were not the least concerned about all that went wrong with the camps. This statement is entirely without foundation and utterly and wilfully false.

*"The Concentration Camps, (1900-1902), Facts, Figures and Tables".

On November 20th 1901, Lord Milner sent a despatch to the Military Governor at Pretoria and to the Deputy Administrator at Bloemfontein.

> As you are aware, the continued high death rate in the concentration camps is causing great anxiety to His Majesty's Government who would evidently shrink from no measures however costly, to mitigate the evil . . . I do not myself believe that the deplorable mortality which has occurred, especially among infants, could by any possibility have been seriously lessened. No doubt the congregation of large numbers of people, including thousands of young children in hastily formed camps, is favourable to the spread of infectious diseases. But during the continuance of the war, the only alternative was to leave the whole non-combatant population to live, or rather to die, in a country denuded of supplies . . . It is clearly the desire of His Majesty's Government that expense should not be allowed to stand in the way, when it is a question of providing anything necessary to improve the health of the camps . . . It would be better to err in the present emergency on the side of liberality than to leave anything unprovided which could promote the health of the inmates of the camps for fear of adding a few thousands to an expenditure which must in any case be heavy.

In an instruction from the General Superintendent, Transvaal Camps, to his subordinates in August 1901, the following appears:

> There must be no stint in the distribution of medical comforts to the sick and also to old and infirm people and young children. When necessary, stimulants may be freely given under doctor's orders. There must always be an adequate supply of milk, which should be liberally supplied to children and deserving people; as well as the sick and convalescent.

Those who, like myself, know a good deal about Hitler's concentration camps, can state without fear of contradiction that Himmler, Heydrich, Kaltenbrunner, and Eichmann never had any qualms at all when as many as 10,000 persons a day were being herded into the gas chambers.

Index